Children in Search of Meaning

This is a study of the primary school years. It draws on
many living children – and on some childhoods in
history – to show that the religious sense is inborn.
Religion begins with everyday discovery by infants, helped
through spoken questions or play. We watch the slow
growth of the power to communicate and to record a
pattern of meaning. Before long a sense of the mysterious
and the 'numinous' in life as a whole can be communi-
cated, perhaps not in words. On such foundations,
human and healthy, a maturer faith in God can be built.

   The whole of Religious Instruction is now being re-
shaped to meet developments in psychological and
theological understanding. This book explores the most
formative period.

   Violet Madge, after much experience in primary
schools, is now a Lecturer at Rolle College, Exmouth.

VIOLET MADGE

Children in Search of Meaning

*A study of religious and scientific thought
and enquiry arising from experience in
the primary school years*

SCM PRESS LTD

Recently published by SCM Press

Sing and Pray
58 Services for Infant or Sunday Schools
Madge Swann

Boys and Girls at Worship
70 Services for Primary or Secondary Schools
R. and E. Doidge

Teenage Religion
Harold Loukes

and its sequel
New Ground in Christian Education
Harold Loukes

First published 1965 by SCM Press Ltd,
56 Bloomsbury Street, London WC1

Printed in Great Britain by
Billing and Sons Ltd,
Guildford and London

Contents

Part Two

SOME REFLECTIONS ON CHILDREN
IN SEARCH OF MEANING

Introduction

Those who made this book possible

THIS BOOK incorporates the goodwill and thoughts of many people. It began when Devon County Education Committee granted me a year's secondment to undertake the Course of Advanced Study for Training College Lecturers at the Leeds University Institute of Education. It was originally submitted as a dissertation at the end of the year's course of full-time study, and is now published by permission of the Institute. Its growth was fostered by teachers, students and parents, who generously shared their experience of childhood, writers whose work stimulated thought and provided comparative material, and children whose very unawareness that they were helping made their contributions invaluable. It was owing to the constructive criticism and persistent spirit of hopefulness of Miss Frances Stevens of Leeds University Institute of Education that the nebulous mass of material, so garnered, took shape.

What this book is about

My original intention in undertaking the study on which this book is based was to consider the interests and religious conceptions of children in the primary school years. I hoped to gather evidence which would enable me to estimate the conceptions fostered by our approach to religious education and to consider whether we sufficiently took into account the spontaneous interests of children. Although the study was initially concerned with religious conceptions, these were soon seen to be clearly associated with scientific ideas, and it seemed important, in an age threatened by a dichotomy of cultures, to consider where integration might take place. The

sense in which the terms 'religious' and 'scientific' are used should
therefore be defined. A statement from the writings of Professor
Jeffreys defines the former:

> Religious truth is normal experience understood at fullest depth;
> what makes truth religious is not that it relates to some abnormal
> field of thought and feeling but that it goes to the roots of the
> experience which it interprets.[1]

'Scientific' is applied not only to the attempt to discover truth
unprejudiced by subjective feelings but also to the mind's effort to
link facts so revealed into an imaginative pattern.

This book is, first, a record of observations of some of the ways
in which children spontaneously seek for meaning in their experience. Some of the questions which such observations raise for
religious education, together with a few references to preparation
for later scientific work, are then discussed.

Lack of time has prevented examination of all the material
collected, and it has not been possible to give detailed consideration
to some of the aspects selected. There are also inevitable omissions:
for example, no illustration is given of how children may use the
media of music and dance as a means of interpretation.

How this book took shape

The material was gathered together in various ways. Whenever
opportunities occurred during my year's secondment personal observations were made of children engaged in spontaneous activities,
but I have also drawn on previous observations made over a period
of years. In addition, I have included some observations contributed
by parents and teachers, as well as recollections of childhood by
adults. The children referred to were from a variety of social and
educational backgrounds, and for the purpose of this book most
have been given fictitious names.[2]

Indirect methods were used whenever possible, especially with
the younger children. An adult using a direct approach can never
be sure that responses are reliable, since young children have a
natural resistance to any attempt to probe their innermost thoughts
and feelings. As Sylvia Anthony commented:

[1] Jeffreys, M. V. C., *Glaucon*, Pitman 1961 edition, p. 118.
[2] This book is based on a variety of observations involving two hundred
children.

The child so approached may close up, like a sea-anemone or a wood-louse; or he may display himself, like a lapwing when her nest is approached, who, of course, does not display her nest but cleverly conceals it.[1]

The investigator must also be careful not to underestimate children's capacity to play up to adult enthusiasms. Anne Treneer's delightful reference to the way in which she and her brother deceived a research worker in the field of folk-lore has therefore been kept in mind:

> Once when we were looking our worst we were in a field where there was an upright granite block—not unlike a monolith, but put there within living memory for cattle to rub against. A pedantic looking tourist brought up in the 'Hodge' tradition asked us about the block. Howard said in broad Cornish that it was called locally the Devil's Poker—it wasn't—and he made up wonderful tales about how it glowed red-hot on Mid-summer night and the piskies danced round. When the person got out a notebook and began to write it all down and said, 'That's most interesting, my man, I'm a collector of local lore. You seem intelligent,' we were in ecstasies. He called me 'little woman'. 'And what do you know about it, little woman?' I gasped out, 'I've zeed the piskies, I 'ave.' For this piece of fantasy Howard gave me a ha-porth of Barcelona balls.[2]

Where more direct, systematic methods have been introduced, as in conversations where I guided the trend of older children's thought, this has been mentioned. I was not entirely happy about such intervention, which proved necessary because time imposed limitations on the scope of my enquiry. It was interesting to note, however, that the ideas expressed in guided discussion corresponded with those revealed in uncontrolled situations: both indicated the limitations which immaturity and lack of experience impose on children's ideas. Ronald Goldman's findings concerning attitudes to religion and science were also endorsed.[3]

What I observed set me reading a variety of books, which, in turn, often enabled me more sensitively to discern the significance of what I had recorded. I have quoted freely from this reading, in

[1] Anthony, Sylvia, *The Child's Discovery of Death*, Kegan Paul 1940, pp. 9-10.
[2] Treneer, Anne, *School House in the Wind*, Jonathan Cape 1950 edition, p. 32.
[3] Goldman, Ronald, *Religious Thinking from Childhood to Adolescence*, Routledge and Kegan Paul 1964, pp. 234-235.

order to set the observations of children against the background of the thought of theologian, psychologist, philosopher, poet and scientist.

The material gathered together in this book was originally a record of a personal quest towards more understanding. It has been suggested that the thinking of others might be quickened by these observations and reflections—however incomplete and imperfect they may be. With such a hope this book is offered to the reader.

PART ONE

Making Discoveries about the World and People

1 *The Infant School Years*

Discovery through spoken questions

PERHAPS THE MOST obvious way in which young children seek
understanding is through the questions which they ask adults and
other children. These make clear children's concern with everyday
situations regarding themselves, other people, and things in their
immediate environment. The following questions, which were asked
of parents and teachers by children from five to seven years of age,
illustrate a search for causes and a keen curiosity about how things
are made:

> How do they make soap?
> How are tears made?
> How do cars go?
> How do ostriches bury their heads in the sand without suffocating?
> How does a cut in your skin heal?
> Do you love me?
> How do buds form on the branches of trees and why are they
> sometimes sticky when they come out?
> How does lightning flash?
> When you light a fire why does smoke come?
> Why do leaves fall off a Christmas tree so quickly?
> How do you make seeds?
> Why do sharks have their mouths on the slope under their chin?
> Sometimes when it rains, it rains on some windows and on other
> windows you find only a few spots. Why?
> How do pips get into apples?

Inherent in a number of the queries is the assumption that 'someone' is responsible for the creation of things:

> Who made the telephones?
> Did God make the curtains?
> Who painted that picture?

An interest in birth and destiny is also evident:

> How do babies come out of their Mummies' tummies?
> How do cows grow calves?
> How was God born?
> How do you die?

In the records I collected specific 'religious' questions asked were few: they tended to appear when the environment fostered such an interest. For example, six year old twins of a minister of religion in America were responsible for the first two queries in the following selection:

> Mummy, in the Bible there is a story about a flood and God promised that there would never be another flood. How come there was a flood in Texas then?
> If Jesus was God, who made Mary?
> Why does Jesus have a Boxing Day after his birthday and we don't?
> How did God make seeds?
> Who is God's Mummy?
> Why can't I see Jesus?
> If God was there before the world was made, what did he walk on?
> If Herod did send the soldiers to the stable, why couldn't the star have led them the wrong way? It was a magic star, wasn't it?
> Why has Jesus got two fathers? Did the other one die?
> Did God die?
> If God came as a spirit, how was he born?
> Does Jesus live inside us or around us?
> Is Jesus God? Is God Jesus' father? How can he be?
> Why can't I hear God's voice inside me like Samuel did?
> Why didn't God make us knowing everything? It would have saved a lot of trouble, wouldn't it?
> Does God have hundreds of eyes so he can see everyone?
> Will Gran have one candle on her cake on her first birthday in heaven? It will be like beginning all over again, won't it?
> How can God possibly make room in heaven for everyone for ever and ever?
> Was it holy before Jesus was born?
> If Jesus is born every Christmas and crucified every Good Friday, how does he grow so quickly?
> Can I give Gran a card to send me when she goes to heaven to tell me what God's face looks like?

A glance at the preceding questions shows how young children interpret new knowledge in terms of already familiar patterns of experience. The effect which both limited experience and stage of mental development have upon children's mode of interpretation can also be discerned. In the query 'Does God have hundreds of eyes?' is seen the assumption that God has human characteristics. There is also evidence of confusion caused by the idea of the divinity of Jesus and the belief in magic so prevalent in the thought of younger children.[1] The question 'If Jesus was God, who made Mary?' recurs frequently throughout the primary school age range. Six year old Edward raised another query with regard to the relationship of God and Jesus in a conversation with a nine year old girl. An adult had been telling the children that no one can always be right:

Hazel	Yes, they can. God can.
Edward	Jesus can, too, and he can be righter than God.
Hazel	No, he can't.
Edward	Who's boss, then, God or Jesus?
Adult	They're both the same.
Hazel	They can't be. God's the father. The father's always the boss.

Anxiety, as well as intellectual curiosity, may be responsible for some enquiries to adults. Mothers have often told me of their children's fear lest mother should die. A child's conversation with his mother illustrates this concern:[2]

Child (4-6)	Mummy, what means a dead mother?
Mother	A woman that has died and does not walk or talk any more.
Child	But what will the children do?
Mother	Well, if a mother should die, the father would take care of them and maybe an aunt.
Child	Will you be a dead mother some day?
Mother	Why yes, though I don't expect to be for a long time.
Child	A *very* long time?
Mother	Yes.
Child	But I don't want you to die; I want you here like this.
Mother	Well you will probably be quite grown up before that happens.

[1] See Appendices B and C for further examples of this characteristic.
[2] Jersild, Arthur, *Child Psychology*, Staples Press 1960, p. 317. (Illustration from M. M. Rust's unpublished thesis: *The Growth of Children's Concepts of Time, Space, and Magnitude*, Teachers College, Columbia University.)

<blockquote>

Child   A *long* time?

Mother Yes.

Child   But what *means* dead, mummy?

Mother Well, your heart stops beating and you lie still without breathing.

Child   And what do you do with the talking part—you know the inside talk?

Mother I'm not sure, but some people think you live in another world, and, of course, some don't.

Child   I guess we do (excitedly). Yes! And then you die in a *long*, long time—a *very* long time, and I die and we both hug each other and then you won't have any wrinkles—Oh, look at that cute pussy. Isn't she darling? (Runs off.)

</blockquote>

The manner in which young children's ideas may also be influenced by asking questions of one another can be seen in five year old Bobby's questioning of John in the book-corner of a nursery school:

Bobby settled in the book-corner and chose a picture book of animals in different countries, becoming intrigued by an African scene depicting a river and jungle country.

'That's a fish,' he told himself, as he looked very intently at the picture. 'There's a monkey. Coo, the monkey's in the water. Crabs and fishes lives in water.'

At this moment John, a very quiet, sensitive five year old from a cultured home, joined Bobby, who was big for his age and rather uncouth. A conversation followed in which Bobby acknowledged and learned from John's authority:

John   Starfish, there too.

Bobby Do they live in water? What else lives in water?

John   I can't think of anything else.

Bobby turned over a page.

Bobby Look, lion (leopard). It is looking through trees, isn't it?

John   There's a crocodile. He's in the water.

Bobby Yes, he's in water. We didn't know what else was in water, did we? Crocodiles in. Now we know, don't we? Crocodiles in water.

Bobby turned over a page.

John　That's an igloo.
Bobby　Igloo. That's an igloo. What are they? Wolves? (dogs drawing sleigh)
John　No, they are dogs.

Bobby turned over a page.

Bobby　What's that?
John　Camel.
Bobby　That's a camel, isn't it? Yes, that's a camel. That's a donkey, that is. Is that a donkey?
John　Yes, that's a donkey.

Sometimes information imparted by other children may cause confusion. A picture of the nursery rhyme *Goosey, Goosey Gander* prompted a conversation about God and prayer among three boys, which caused the five year old some distress: [1]

Ben (8:6)　And *you* don't say *your* prayers, Richard!
Richard (5:4)　I don't know what it means.
Ben　A thing you say to God.
Robert (7:6)　What you say to God at night, isn't it, Ben?
Richard　But I don't know what God is (distressed).
Ben　God's a thing that isn't really (laughing). At least, that's what I think, only I pray to Him. A kind of imaginary thing that floats about in the air. At least, that's what I think!

A few other observations made by teachers of children in their class-rooms show how a spontaneous interchange of query and answer may arise:

During the morning an aeroplane flew rather low over school and Andrew, aged five years, queried: 'I wonder if the man in that aeroplane can see us?'
Donald, aged six, standing nearby, replied: 'Well, he might, but he might think we are very small, but we are not really.'

A group of six and seven year olds were modelling 'cakes' from dough for their class-room shop. A five year old onlooker, after feeling and comparing the soft dough with the models made some weeks previously, enquired: 'How does it get hard?'

[1] Anthony Sylvia, *The Child's Discovery of Death*, Kegan Paul 1940, p. 175.

Carl, aged seven, explained rather scornfully: 'Fresh air, of course, it dries it up.'

'Fresh air, fresh air,' commented the five year old.

Martin and David, aged seven years, were drawing, when Martin enquired of David: 'How can I draw a train going fast and make it look as though it is moving fast?'

'I painted a racing car passing some people and I painted a grey cloud of dust blowing over the people watching. You might do something like that,' David suggested.

But there are times when the questions asked apparently have no direct connection with the activities in which the children are engaged. This occurred when six year old Simon and a friend were playing with trains. Simon was overheard by his mother to answer his friend's query about where babies come from with the explanation: 'God sprinkles packets of baby seeds down from heaven, and sometimes ladies catch them and they have babies, and sometimes they fall on the earth and become flowers.' A group of five year olds were overheard discussing the question of destiny in the midst of modelling with plasticine:

Sheena	When you die you go to heaven, don't you?
Vivian	Yes, but you go in a coffin first.
Sheena	What's a coffin?
Vivian	(indicating with her hands) A big long box, big enough to put you in, and they put you under the ground and later you go to heaven.
Denise	How do you get to heaven?
Sheena	Oh, by aeroplane, I suppose.
Vivian	(indignantly) No, you are silly.
Denise	Well, how?
Vivian	Well, you just do.

The interests and characteristics noted in the enquiries addressed to adults are also reflected in these questions to their peers. The part experience plays is evident in replies like that of Carl about the effect of air on the dough. Simon's speculative attempt to deal with his friend's query in terms of his limited knowledge is typical of the way in which young children are constantly trying to make sense out of what they know.

Exploring the world around

Although verbal questions are certainly one way in which children reach out for understanding, such enquiries inevitably spring from the child's predominating mode of discovery through action. This may be seen in simple speculative behaviour involving sensory experience and physical movement in which, though questions may not be voiced, they are implicit. As five year old Paul experimented with the sand he seemed to be posing and answering such questions as: What will happen if I do this? Will it happen if I do it again?

Paul used his hands to make a small mound of sand. He took a wooden rod and pushed it in the middle of the mound, patting the sand with his hands to make it firm. He removed the rod rather roughly, which caused the sand to fall into the space vacated by the rod.

He then re-made the mound with his hands, but patted it with a small spade *before* he placed the rod in the centre. He tapped the top of the rod with his spade, causing the mound of sand to fall apart and the rod to topple over.

Finally, he repeated the second performance, with the exception of tapping the top of the rod, and then very cautiously and gently he removed it, leaving the sand mound intact. Carefully he re-inserted the rod in the mound of sand before wandering off to another occupation.

Similar reactions may be noted in a group of four and five year olds who had been introduced to water-play in school for the first time. But on this occasion the play was stimulated by the presence of other children and, unlike Paul, some of these children sought to clarify their experience in the language of words as well as action. The motion of scooping up the water reminded David of the fish and chip shop and, quite oblivious to other children's activities, he, at one point, seemed to use the water as a means of trying to understand what it must feel like to be 'the fish and chip lady'. The children, with the exception of Roger, who continued with his own interest, politely listened to the adult suggestion that the water might be used to make discoveries of another kind. But immediately afterwards they all reverted to their own personal explorations.

Ann, Barbara, David and Roger chose to play with water in a large zinc bath. Each child took a jug and immersed it in the water, then emptied the water back into the zinc bath. Ann noticed a larger jug on a nearby table and quickly grabbed it. Placing it on the table by the zinc bath she emptied the water out of her own jug into it. The other three children then imitated her and poured water from their jugs into the larger one.

The teacher passing by paused to suggest: 'What about seeing how many of these little jugs of water it takes to fill this large one? Watch me and I will show you. Count.'

The children responded to the request to count, except Roger who was busy giving his absorbed attention to the behaviour of the water as he dipped his hands in and out of it. As soon as the teacher passed on, the children continued to fill and empty the jugs in a haphazard fashion. After a while, Ann observed: 'We've got a lot of water haven't we? We've lost some. We've not really. Look it is here.' This remark was accompanied by chuckles as Ann indicated the large jug which the children had filled with water from the zinc bath.

The children continued to repeat the process of filling their jugs with water, emptying them into the large jug until it was full, urged on by Ann: 'Come on, let's fill it right to the top,' she said, '*right* to the *top*.'

Some very crude attempts at co-operation and self-control were involved as the three children engaged in the effort of filling the large jug, but the self-discipline was spasmodic and broke down at the least provocation. At one point the three jugs clashed over the opening of the large jug and there was a tussle before the children realized that they could not empty their jugs into the large one unless one of them gave way: Barbara was the one who obliged.

David later picked up a half pint jug and filling and emptying it in an indiscriminate fashion commented: 'I'm the fish and chip lady.' He continued his 'fish and chip' play for nine minutes, commenting from time to time: 'I'm the fish and chip lady.'

Roger was the first to tire of the water-play. He went off to find his teacher, telling her: 'I'm not going to play with that wet stuff!'

The exploration of the nature and possibilities of objects in the environment, as well as raw materials, is a well-known characteristic manifestation of children's curiosity and may be illustrated by their reactions to several different situations in which man-made objects were being examined.

The first concerns a miniature toy model car which I introduced to a group of five and six year olds. The children's first response was to comment on their own similar possessions. They then started to play with the toy, pushing it to one another, remarking on its speed and making an appropriate sound of 'Zzzz' as they propelled it across the floor. One of the children then picked it up and started to examine it more closely, pointing out to me: 'Look it's got wheels on it.'

When I enquired: 'What else do you know about cars?' the remarks which ensued included:

Ivan	Cars come from a garage, don't they?
Steven	Yes, they need petrol.
Paul	They need oil so they don't get rusty.
Celia	Yes, they make cars out of iron, then they paints them and puts handles on.
Steven	They need some wires.
James	They got to have tyres.
Karen	And they have to have a boot.
Celia	They have to have a thing that tells you how fast it goes.
Kathryn	I know what, they got a steering wheel.
Steven	It's got an engine. They need windows, too.
Ivan	They makes toy cars out of plastic. I think they make the plastic out of cement.
Miss M.	Who makes the real cars?
Steven	The garage men, they make them.
Paul	They gets some iron and roll it with their hands.
Judith	Yes, and they roll it into the shape of a car, the misters do.
Mary	Misters! Silly, you mean men.

These reactions to an object, in common with those registered in the next two observations, represent children's natural urge to explore possibilities by action and the way in which they relate the new experience to previously acquired experience and knowledge. Ivan's suggestion that plastic might be made from cement is a typical momentary speculation, whilst Paul's reference to the fact that iron was rolled out in men's hands to make cars seems likely to have been conditioned by the fact that he had been modelling with plasticine immediately before joining the group.

A second observation shows children's curiosity about objects which act in an unusual manner. A few magnets were introduced to six five year olds, who had previously seen their teacher use a magnet but had not personally handled them. The children sat on the floor, examining the contents of two boxes, one containing magnets, the other a variety of articles (rubber, wood, paper, etc.). Left free to investigate with no adult interference, four of the children remained engrossed for nearly half an hour, having to be interrupted to 'go out to play'. There was considerable excitement at first as the children made random experiments, most of them making a running commentary on the proceedings, which consisted of such remarks as:

It picked that up.
It won't pick this up.
I've got two things up, I have.
Ooh, I've got these nails up with the big magnet.
It's picked up more than one; lots of nails.
Look, Miss M. . . . look at me. Look!
Gosh, these have got stuck together (two magnets).

Gradually the excitement subsided and two children became absorbed in problems which presented themselves. Patrick discovered that one magnet attracted another. He laid the horseshoe magnet over a straight one, discovering that it was only when one magnet touched a certain part of another that 'attraction' took place. For five minutes he experimented with the two magnets in this way, making no comment.

Sally, who recalled a demonstration given by an adult, asked me to hold a piece of paper on which she had placed some nails. She then moved a magnet to and fro under the paper. 'Look, Miss M. . . .,' she exclaimed with amazement, 'They're wriggling, aren't they? I'm making them wriggle.'

At one point excitement caused Sally to move the magnet roughly, scattering the nails on the floor. 'Stupid things,' she muttered, as she retrieved the nails. Replacing them on the paper she continued her experimental activity with greater control.

David tried to imitate Sally and after initial failure, announced in exasperation: 'They don't wriggle. Mine don't wriggle.' By further trial and error, however, he discovered that the magnet had to be directly under the nails to achieve the desired result.

Donald paused and watched before enquiring: 'How do you do that?'

Sally gave a demonstration, explaining: 'You put it under the paper and they wriggle like this. But you must be careful 'cos they will get knocked off.'

It was Donald, who, a week later, provided an example of how young children may be inwardly endeavouring to relate one experience to another, when he suggested to me that perhaps the angels used a magnet to make the clouds move along.

The next observation of five year old Colin's absorption in the possibilities of activities with a bucket, which lasted for half an hour, is an example of the painstaking ingenuity a child may exercise in self-initiated research on objects he encounters:

> Colin stood on the second rung of an indoor climbing frame, holding the end of a piece of string, the other end of which was tied to the handle of a small bucket. He gathered up the piece of string, placing it in the bucket, so that he could hold the handle and ascend several more rungs. He then lowered the bucket into the space on the other side of the rungs by letting the string slip through his fingers very slowly. After a moment's contemplation he let the string fall from his hands before climbing down the rungs to the floor.
> Colin then placed the bucket on the floor by the side of the climbing frame and standing on a chair passed the string through a pulley on the end of the climbing frame and behind two metal discs fixed to a connecting bar. After removing the chair, he then pulled the string up and down, his eyes being intent on the movement of the bucket at the other end. When, owing to his jerky movements, the string slipped from behind one of the discs on the bar, he carefully replaced it and continued the action of pulling it along and suddenly releasing it.
> After a while the sight of the door handle seemed to give Colin another idea, for he wound the string around it. The first time when he let the string go the weight of the bucket at the other end pulled the string from behind the discs. Once again Colin replaced the string behind the discs and re-wound it round the door handle more securely than on the previous occasion. He then more cautiously released his hold of the string. Standing back he observed the effect of this revised procedure, and turning to an observer sitting nearby he smiled as he realized the success of his experiment.

Colin's patient experiments were not accompanied by any spoken remarks, but it was obvious that through the opportunity of experimental action knowledge was not only being ordered but re-ordered in the light of experience. This was seen when he discovered that in order to counterbalance the weight of the bucket it was necessary to secure the string round the door handle more firmly. Christopher, however, in the next observation indicated by spoken comment that his action had reinforced the effect of previous rough handling of utensils containing water.

> Christopher, not yet five, experimented with a rope which had been placed through a pulley fixed in an archway of the playroom,

a bucket being attached to one end of the string. He stood on a chair and pulled the string through the pulley until the bucket came to the top, whereupon he released the string quickly, causing the bucket to bump on the floor. He repeated this experiment twice, then pulling up the bucket so that it was suspended near the pulley at the top of the archway he observed: 'It's too high up to reach now. No one could reach it now. Miss . . . couldn't reach it now. If the bucket was full of water the water would splash out all over, wouldn't it, if I banged it down like that?'

Watching children engaged in such purposeful, absorbing self-initiated activity made one aware of the truth of Nathan Isaacs' reminder that the child is the architect of his intellectual growth, and that this '. . . rests on the principle of continuous *interaction* between the child and the world around him; it is this that furnishes all the material, as well as the motive force for his intellectual advance'.[1]

A child's curiosity about the world around him will also bring him into contact with creatures and plants. This curiosity may sometimes appear to take destructive forms, as the young child does not appreciate the effects of his explorations. Robert, prompted by the urge to handle, removed some stones placed in a bowl of water to support growing plants. His dominant interest at that moment was what he could do with the stones and water, rather than in the growing flowers.

That we may be unaware of the impact of experiences we provide may be illustrated by Robin. Newly arrived at school, he spoke little, but had chosen to plant some wheat seeds. His initial reaction shows a lack of time sense, characteristic of young children, but unlike Robert he controlled his urge to probe. It was his mother who reported that at 2.0 a.m. the night after the seeds had been planted she was awakened by her young son coming into her bedroom to enquire if she thought the seeds he had planted in school the previous day would be grown when he arrived the next morning. Robin learned of the time needed for growth to take place as day by day he examined the bowl, occasionally disturbing the soil with his fingers. The morning Robin discovered the shoots appearing above the earth his excitement caused him to break through his usual reserve as he exclaimed loudly: 'Come here, *look*, Miss M., *look*.'

[1] Isaacs, Nathan, *The Growth of Understanding in Young Children*, ESA 1961, p. 7.

Such experiences may be of the utmost intensity:

There was a child went forth every day,
And the first object he look'd upon, that object he became,
And that object became part of him for the day or a certain part of
    the day,
Or for many years or stretching cycles of years.
The early lilacs became part of this child,
And grass and white and red morning glories and white and red
    clover, and the song of the phoebe bird,
And the third month lambs and the sow's pink faint litter, and the
    mare's foal and the cow's calf,
And the noisy brood of the barnyard or by the mire of the pond side,
And the fish suspending themselves so curiously below there, and the
    beautiful curious liquid,
And the water-plants with their graceful flat heads, all became part
    of him . . .[1]

Whitman, the poet, perceived the vital contribution contacts with
the natural world may make to a child's growth. The importance of
such contacts was also stressed by Froebel, who believed that
familiarity with Nature in childhood might lay the foundations of
literary, mathematical, scientific and religious study.[2]

Discovery through construction

The curiosity which prompts a child to investigate the possibilities
of raw materials and objects may also lead to constructive efforts,
Paul's sand-building being a simple example (p. 19). Three five
year old boys playing with bricks also show how problem-solving
may be involved in a constructive activity.

> Three five year old boys building with a road-set decided to make
> some bridges over the roads with wooden bricks. Having made a
> bridge with three bricks they found that when they pushed their cars
> under it the bridge collapsed because it was too narrow. The bridge
> was rebuilt several times with the same result and tempers began
> to fray.
> Mark exclaimed with exasperation: *'Why* does this silly bridge
> keep falling down? It is spoiling our game.'
> John thought it would be a good idea to do without a bridge, but
> Stuart, who had been watching silently, had worked out the problem

[1] Whitman, Walt, *Complete Verse and Selected Poems,* Nonesuch Press
1938.
[2] Froebel, Friedrich *The Education of Man*, Appleton N.Y., 1887.

in his mind, for he suggested: 'Why don't you use a longer brick for the top of the bridge?'

This suggestion was tried out and the boys, discovering that the cars then passed under the bridge with ease, continued their game happily.

Scrap materials, together with appropriate tools, may also suggest to young children constructive ventures in which problems are encountered. A few observations indicate children's responses to such situations and how they arrived at solutions.

Michael, like primitive man (and indeed civilized man in many everyday situations) when faced with the question of measurement, can be seen to be content with self-originated measuring techniques of a crude and approximate nature. In the early years children tend to rely on visual comparison, and later, as in the case of Michael, objects are actually placed alongside each other for comparative purposes. Professor Piaget referred to this development as that of 'visual' to 'manual' transfer, when '. . . although the comparison is still visual, it is no longer comparison at a distance, but an appraisal of a whole, made up of neighbouring objects'.[1] New possibilities then present themselves in children's explorations.

Five year old Michael arrived at the Nursery one morning and examined a steamer he had made from scrap materials the previous day. 'I'm going to make a bridge for it,' he announced as he set the steamer down and went to a work-table on the other side of the room.

He selected a large empty Oxydol carton from the junk box and with the aid of scissors he proceeded to cut the front section away before he cut out an archway on either side of the carton.

Several times he glanced over at the boat to make a visual comparison of the archway and the steamer. This way of checking apparently did not altogether satisfy him, for he eventually took the bridge over to the steamer. He then discovered that the archway was neither high enough for the funnel to pass under, nor wide enough to permit the ship to pass through. An adult nearby, noticing his predicament, enquired: 'What must you do, Michael?'

Michael replied: 'I must make it wider and higher,' and went back to the table to resume cutting operations. Comparing the bridge with the boat a second time he observed: 'Still not high enough, I'll make another one.'

---

[1] Piaget, Jean, *The Child's Conception of Geometry*, Routledge and Kegan Paul 1960, p. 31.

Michael then took a cornflakes carton, but after comparing it with the bridge made from the Oxydol carton he rejected it in favour of a Daz carton which was of identical size. It appeared that at this point he decided not to carry out his first intention of enlarging the archway of his original bridge. Instead, he made two more bridges similar to the first one, using the latter as his model.

Michael experienced considerable difficulty in manipulating his scissors, but because mastery of the skill was necessary to reach his goal he struggled to achieve it.

The three bridges completed, Michael took them over to the table and compared them with his steamer. He seemed aware of, but unperturbed by, the fact that the archways were not large enough for the steamer to pass through and sang quietly to himself in a rhythmic fashion: 'You can't go under the bridge. You can't go under the bridge. No, you *can't* go under the bridge.'

As experience is gained and mental development takes place, children will face and solve problems of a more complex nature with increasing attention to precision. Seven year old Rachel, having decided to make a windmill from scrap materials, spent four free choice periods in school, each of an hour and a half, completely absorbed in the problems which arose. Discussion with other children occurred about how to make the sails go round, necessitating the discipline of communicating ideas through the symbol of the spoken word. Great was her delight when she finally achieved her objective: placing a stick through a circular cardboard carton and tying two pieces of cane together in criss-cross fashion, she then fastened them with wool to the projecting stick. These processes called for the exercise of reasoning and imagination as Rachel, revaluating her work, made decisions as to the best materials, tools and techniques for the solution of her problems.

Discovery about people

Any reference to a child's discovery of people must start with mention of the way in which he comes to a growing awareness of himself. Jean Paul Richter recalls the strong impact of this realization when, as a very young child, he stood one afternoon at the house door and 'All at once that inward consciousness *I am* a ME came like a flash of lightning from Heaven. . . .'[1]

[1] Quoted by Walter de la Mare in *Early One Morning*, Faber and Faber 1935, p. 171.

Wordsworth relates how this awareness of self may be seen in a child's joy in his physical being. He remembers how

> . . . many a time have I, a five years' child,
> In a small mill-race severed from his stream,
> Made one long bathing of a summer's day;
> Basked in the sun, and plunged and basked again
> Alternate, all a summer's day, or scoured
> The sandy field, leaping through flowery groves
> Of yellow ragwort; or when rock and hill,
> The woods, the distant Skiddaw's lofty height,
> Were bronzed with deepest radiance, stood alone
> Beneath the sky, as if I had been born
> On Indian plains, and from my mother's hut
> Had run abroad in wantonness, to sport
> A naked savage, in the thunder shower.[1]

Two four year olds, in a similar joy and absorption in their own physical being, give evidence that the poet's description is an authentic memory. They remind us that young children are very new to themselves; that they need time and opportunity to come to a realization of self as well as other people and the world about them.

> Jill and Susan sat together on a low bench, swaying to and fro from the hips upwards, singing in rhythmic fashion: '*Oh*, oh, oh; *Oh*, oh, oh; *Oh*, oh, oh.'
> The first '*Oh*' of each trio was emphasized, the following two said in quiet tones. This experimental procedure with body and voice continued for five minutes, then Jill got up and danced around, Susan following her example. After a few moments they joined hands and danced together, finally falling over and chuckling with delight. Momentary rough and tumble play ensued before they both got up, each dancing around on her own before going off to another activity.

As happened to Jill and Susan, children through activities in which they discover themselves become involved in problems of relationships with other people. This could be seen in Ann's leadership of the water-play and the need for self-control which became apparent in the co-operative attempt at filling one jug (p. 20). It was also evident in the discipline demanded in the communication of ideas by demonstration and the spoken word in the play with magnets (p. 22) and Rachel's discussion with her friends about the

[1] Wordsworth, William, *The Prelude*, Book 1, 288-300, J. M. Dent, 1940 edition.

difficulties of making her windmill (p. 27). An observation of five and six year olds shows how they solved problems of a social nature.

A group of six year olds were modelling with dough. Five year old Dawn, who badly wanted to join in, tried to take some of Sarah's dough. Sarah did not want to share her dough and tried to restrain Dawn. After a while Sarah solved the problem by giving Dawn a minute portion of the dough, and drawing a line across the floury table with her finger she said very crossly: 'There you are, you use that part of the table and don't you dare to cross this line.'

As well as entering into the problems associated with co-operation with their peers, children may also use the medium of play to enter into the role of other people, as was seen in David's use of the water-play situation when he identified himself with the 'fish and chip lady' (p. 20). Four year old Jonathan who, according to his teacher, was at the time of the next observation 'very absorbed in the feminine side of life', was also engaged in an imitative activity of an adult.

Having wrestled with the difficulties of putting up the ironing board in the Wendy House, Jonathan then spent twenty-five minutes deeply engrossed in the action of ironing every available scrap of fabric he could lay his hands on. Each article was meticulously smoothed out, ironed and folded before Jonathan placed it in a neat pile on a chair he had provided for the purpose.

At the same time in the opposite corner of the Wendy House, Keith was trying out an adult role as he held a conversation with an imaginary person on the toy telephone.

'Aye? What was it you said? All right, Sir. I will, Sir. Oh, hello, Daddy. Oh, yes, certainly. This is my sister you know. Let me see, have you met her? Speak to him.'
The last command was addressed to Carol standing nearby, who took the receiver in her hand and said: 'Hello,' before handing it back to Keith. Keith then brought the one-sided conversation to an end by saying: 'Goodbye, Daddy. Cheerio, darling. Hullo, Daddy, are you still there? Will you bring some cornflakes with you when you come back? Cheerio for now.'

The Deity may sometimes figure in dramatic play. In her book *Exploring the Child's World* Helen Parkhurst writes of how a two and a half year old boy in an American nursery played out the role of God as Creator as, standing on a chair, he announced 'I'm God and I just borned everybody'.[1] Herbert Palmer recalls in his autobiography how he, too, integrated his conception of God into his play-life.

> One of my greatest nursery joys was building houses with wooden bricks and I specially liked to play what I called 'a snowy day'. This was done by powdering rock soda or alum from a nutmeg-grater over my little towns. As I scraped, and the white dust fell tablewards, I imagined myself to be God and His angels dispensing white purity over town-dwellers, and when after half an hour's industry the whole fabric of streets and wooden houses was thoroughly overspread, I was in a transport of self-admiration. The white covering would be trodden by little dolls and Noah's Ark animals, and after I had ploughed it into what I imagined to be slush from innumerable beating feet I would improvise a raging snow-shower to cover up all the unevenness.[2]

Marjorie Hourd observed that 'Dramatization is at once the means by which the child ventures out into the characters and lives of others, and the means by which he draws these back as symbols into the person of himself'.[3]

A study of children's dramatic play indicates how they may be wrestling with conceptions of such mysteries as birth and death. Sometimes such ideas may be dramatized in a straightforward manner, as when six year old Richard commanded me to 'go dead', signifying that I should lie down and close my eyes. After a few moments he announced: 'You can come alive now.' But the resurrection was shortlived for within moments I was commanded to 'go dead' again. Then roles were exchanged, as Richard lay on the floor with closed eyes instructing me to make him come alive. Two children, who lived on a farm, were observed enacting the birth of puppies which they had recently witnessed. The boy, aged five years, said to his five year old girl companion: 'You lie down and I'll crawl out of your tummy and be borned.'

There are occasions, however, when young children are engaged in working over problems which are unvoiced and dimly perceived. Gwendolen Freeman appreciated that '. . . the greatest disadvan-

---

[1] Parkhurst, Helen, *Exploring the Child's World*, Appleton-Century Crofts Inc. N.Y. 1951, p. 208.
[2] Palmer, Herbert E., *The Mistletoe Child*, J. M. Dent 1953, pp. 80-81.
[3] Hourd, Marjorie, *The Education of the Poetic Spirit*, Heinemann 1949, p. 26.

tage is that you are alone. You don't tell anything about yourself—anything of importance. You are inwardly incoherent anyhow.'[1] Sympathetic observation may unveil some of children's problems and suggest that they are in their own way constantly striving to achieve an inner coherence. They mingle fantasy and reality in their dramatic play in an attempt to sort out impressions and '. . . the observer is aware of an intense inner life being externalized in these play activities'.[2] This was apparent as a group of five year olds played with sand.

Catherine	Let's make a witch's castle.
Julia	Yes, let's make a witch's castle.
Catherine	Come on, let's make the castle with flower beds around it and walls around it. Hurry up, the witch will be cross.
Rosemary	I'm going to make the witch's castle look pretty.
Catherine	We will make her a beautiful castle.
Alan	We will make her a beautiful castle, then the witch won't be cross with us or hit us. I will put on my magic hat. (Pretends to put hat on head.)
Catherine	I've got mine on.
Rosemary	Yes, we've all got magic hats on.
Julia	So have I.
Catherine	Come on, the witch will be here soon. We must get her house ready.
Alan	Hurry up, she is coming down the garden path. (The children look around the room and 'see' her coming.)
Catherine	She is coming along the lane. She is quite far. She will take plenty of time. It will take her half an hour to get along, the time she is taking, she will.
Alan	Perhaps it is a man witch.
Julia	I will make the doorway.
Catherine	She can come right through if we make the door the other side, can't she? This is the little archway in the witch's castle, this is.
Alan	(looking around the room) Ooh, she's at the garden gate.
Rachel	(in a very deep voice) I am coming to live in your house.
Catherine	(makes a growling sound) That's a sound of husbands, isn't it? We will turn her into a pig if she is nasty, shall we?

[1] Freeman, Gwendolen, *Children Never Tell*, Allen and Unwin 1949, p. 154.
[2] Hourd, Marjorie, op. cit., p. 25.

Julia	Yes, we will (jumps and waves her hands). There, she is a pig. Now turn her back into a witch (waves her hands again).
Rachel	Let's make it into a queen's castle.
Catherine	Queens don't have castles.
Julia	Yes, they do. They have moats.
Alan	Queens have coaches, don't they, Miss M . . . ?
Catherine	One day an owl bit the witch. The witch was cross and took all the conkers off the owl's best conker trees. The witch is very cross. She is going to saw him up for dinner. I love owls, don't you. Isn't it a shame?
Alan	Let's turn the witch into a kangaroo (waves hands). There's she's a kangaroo.
Julia	Do you know she has bit my hat off. She is very naughty, and I do not like her for that.
Catherine	Neither do I, nasty thing.
Rosemary	No, we won't make her a lovely castle.
Alan	(to adult) Come and touch our castle. Be careful, though, because it's magic. Anything might happen.
Rosemary	Let's pretend she is a kind witch, shall we?
Catherine	All right, we will. Shall I cut her up?
Rosemary	No, she is a kind witch now.
Julia	No, she is a horrible witch, isn't she?
Catherine	Oh, come along, let's go and see the owl. (Catherine and Rosemary opens a cupboard door.)
Catherine	Careful she is looking after the owlets.
Alan	Tu-whit, tu-whoo, tu-whit, tu-whoo.

The strong feelings of aggression and fear projected into this play-situation remind us of Susan Isaacs' suggestion that such activities appear to make it '. . . easier for the child to control his real behaviour and to accept the limitations of the real world'.[1]

Miniature aeroplane models combined with brick building also provided an opportunity for a group of six and seven year olds to think through questions of right and wrong, and suggested that seven year old Graham was becoming conscious of the meaning of 'being fair'. His suggestion that if they built castles for the 'bad side' then the 'good side' could legitimately knock them down was an interesting solution to a moral problem. Angus's 'bad leg' was of special interest, too, since it occurred shortly after his sister had broken her leg, which inevitably focused attention on her. The satis-

[1] Isaacs, Susan, *The Intellectual Growth of Young Children*, Routledge and Kegan Paul 1948 edition, p. 102.

faction Angus gained through this play was obvious and illustrated how a child may manipulate co-operative play to work out a private problem.

Angus	This aeroplane is ready for the fight in the war.
Sandra	Let's pretend it belongs to our American friends. We will pretend there is a war coming on, shall we?
Graham	Yes, let's do that.
Angus	Bang. This aeroplane is going to drop a bomb. Let's pretend it's wartime.
Graham	Who is on the bad side?
Angus	I am. I'm a wounded soldier. I fight in the battle fight. My leg is bad, very bad. I'll have a stick. It's in plaster. (Angus walked around the room limping, obviously enjoying the attention of the others.)
Sandra	Poor Angus.
Angus	Yes, it is a bad leg. I've got a gun. It's a long war, it will go on until next year.
Sandra	I know I am on the right side.
Graham	I'll tell you what, we'll all build castles for the bad side, then it won't matter if *we* knock them down.

Five year old Ian, unaware that he was observed, illustrated in his solitary game of pretence how a young child may integrate what appear unrelated experiences and immediate needs into his fantasy thinking. Sunday school instruction, a recollection of a recent wireless account of the launching of an American rocket and aggressive feelings towards his older sisters became woven into his thought-pattern on this occasion.

Ian came home from Sunday school. Displaying and unrolling a piece of paper which had been fastened to two spills, he announced: 'I've got a scroll book.'

Re-rolling the scroll he quickly converted it into a gun, and accompanied by appropriate actions and the sound of 'bang, bang, bang' he in turn 'shot' each of the three adults in the room. Then he sat down and played with a constructive toy, singing to himself as he did so, 'Kingdom glory, kingdom glory' over and over again.

Tiring of his constructive efforts he fetched a paper aeroplane and holding it aloft he counted backwards with considerable difficulty, '10, 9, 8, 7, 6, 5, 4, 3, 2, 1, *Zero*', and his plane became airborne. After this he found a paper boat, and murmured to himself as he played with it: 'This is the Holy Spirit's boat. The Holy Spirit has a gun.'

B

He paused for a moment while he placed a strip of rolled paper into the boat to form a gun. 'Bang, bang, bang,' he exclaimed, 'That's the Holy Spirit's gun. I'll tell God to kill you two.'

The last remark was addressed to his two older sisters who had just reprimanded him for being untidy and noisy.

Discovery through communicating and recording

(a) *The spoken word*

The foregoing observations give evidence of the way in which, whilst engaged in all manner of activities, young children may come to realize the significance of the spoken word as a means of communication. Sometimes they can be overheard merely commenting to themselves, little concerned whether there is a response from others, as Jeremy did when painting his picture (p. 38). At other times they will deliberately endeavour to communicate both their enquiries and the nature of their needs or conceptions to others through the medium of the spoken word. This interchange of words will be incidental and frequently for pragmatic purposes, being closely related to immediate matters. But, as in instances quoted, children may declare in words their mistaken or half-formed ideas, revealing their need for experience or knowledge, or indicating the effect of premature instruction. Spontaneous comment may also reveal the way in which children try to integrate the impressions gained from their experiences. A four year old daughter of a clergyman, when playing 'mothers and fathers' with a friend, who had declared her intention of being the mother, stated emphatically that she was going to be 'The Father, Son and Holy Ghost'.

Sylvia Anthony records a conversation between a mother and her six year old son, which illustrates the same point.

Ben	Why can't you keep cream to the next day?
Mother	Because it goes bad. Most things do that have been alive; if you don't eat them soon, you can't eat them at all.
Ben	Do you think when we die we go up to the shops in Heaven, and then God buys us and puts us in his larder and eats us?[1]

A more extended example occurred when Lucy, aged nearly five, wove phrases she had heard in everyday conversation into the Christmas story as she described the picture of the Nativity to her

[1] Anthony, Sylvia, *The Child's Discovery of Death*, Kegan Paul, ch. IV.

doll. 'I'll sing you a song about that,' she said. Her mother wrote down the song verbatim:[1]

> When the baby borned
> Joseph said to Mary
> 'What am I going to do about
> This little-born Jesus baby Christ?
> I never knew it was going to be like this
> With all these angels and kings
> And shepherds and stars and things.
> It's got me worried, I can tell you
> On Christmas Day in the morning.'
>
> Mary said to Joseph
> 'Not to worry, my darling,
> Dear old darling Joseph,
> Everything's going to be all right,
> Because the angel told me not to fear;
> So just hold up the lamp
> So I can see the dear, funny, sweet, little face
> Of my darling little-born Jesus, baby Christ.'
>
> Joseph said to Mary,
> 'Behold the handyman of the Lord.'
>
> Happy Christmas, Happy Christmas,
> Christ is born today.

On occasion young children's verbal expression may represent their inner grappling with puzzling and complex ideas concerning, for example, human relationships. In her study of the imagination of young children Ruth Griffiths quotes a striking example. She records how a five year old boy, Dick, told her a series of stories in which he appeared to be attempting to resolve problems connected with the conception of possession.[2] Such an example suggests the important role which fantasy may take in a child's search for meaning. Ruth Griffiths herself puts it thus:

> Imagination is, in fact, the child's method not so much of avoiding the problems presented by environment, but of overcoming those

---

[1] From *Home and Family*, December 1963.
[2] Griffiths, Ruth, *A Study of Imagination in Early Childhood*, Routledge and Kegan Paul 1935, ch. X.

difficulties in a piecemeal and indirect fashion, returning again and again to a problem and gradually developing a socialized attitude which finally finds expression at the level of overt action and adapted behaviour.[1]

Although the function of fantasy seems particularly important to children with deep-rooted problems a glance at some of the preceding observations indicates that it is a natural means whereby all children seek to work over their ideas, which may sometimes find expression in words in the midst of play (see sand-play, p. 32). But sometimes children formulate a clearer pattern in their interpretation. Six year old Sheila did this at a time when she was preoccupied with the idea of 'naughtiness' and its consequences. Her thoughts were expressed in a series of stories she told to me concerning the misdeeds of some puppies, of which this is one:

> Once upon a time there were three little dogs and they played in the grass, which was near their favourite tree. They played around it often. One day these naughty little dogs ran into the house and one little dog fetched two little balls. The other dog fetched two bubble pipes. They went out on to the green grass and began tossing these bubble pipes into the air, and they fell down and broke. The three little dogs ran into the house and hid and they waited until the other dog came in, but it was a long time before the other dog came in. Then she came. She was their mother and she began hunting for her three little dogs after she had found the broken bubble pipes on the grass where they had been playing. Then the mother found them and she was very cross with them indeed.

There may also be occasions when a young child's verbal interpretations of experience may embody his spontaneous wonder and seem to '. . . . contain like the myths of primitive man, a germ of true thought'.[2] Alison, the sensitive five year old daughter of highly intelligent agnostics, came to school one morning and, seeking me, confided quietly:

> In the night I close my eyes and I think of stories to tell you. Last night I thought of this one. A little girl lived in the sky. The sun was shining. She said: 'I like the sun. I like the sun. I am going to praise to it.' You see she wanted to praise the sun because it was shining bright.

[1] *A Study of Imagination in Early Childhood*, p. 354.
[2] Sully, *Studies of Childhood*, Longmans 1896, p. 61.

Children feel the urge to formulate their thoughts into a pattern of spoken words at quite unpredictable times. It may come to a child in the midst of activity, as it did when five year old Adrian, who, playing with a group of boys building an aerodrome with bricks on the classroom floor, parted momentarily from his peers to find me. Brick in one hand he requested: 'Please can I tell you a story?' The story was about a little aeroplane to whom, in the manner of young children, Adrian attributed human thought and feeling.

Once upon a time there was a little aeroplane, and he used to carry a lot of people and he would fly a long way and then have a little rest. And sometimes after breakfast he went for a long trip and then came home again.

One day he suddenly saw an aerodrome below him and he said: 'Oh, I would love to go there.' So he came down and he met lots of big aeroplanes and he made friends with lots of aeroplanes. And when it was tea-time he flew back home.

A pony she had made out of newspaper stimulated six year old Annette to break out into rhyme. She had painted the pony with multi-coloured spots—'because he is a magic pony'—and christened him Spotty. Holding the creature in one hand she moved him along the table top with rhythmical trotting movements, singing softly a rhyme which seemed to have come to her mind in the moment of action:

> Spotty, Spotty,
> Trotting down the lane,
> Spotty, Spotty,
> In the pouring rain
>
> In a little minute
> Out will come the sun
> Spotty, Spotty,
> He's having lots of fun.

(b) *Picture-making and the spoken word*

The language of words may also accompany children's picture-making, itself a popular medium through which children seek to clarify experience, as illustrated by five year old Maurice and Jeremy.

These two boys stood at the nursery window one morning silently watching the falling snow. Later in the morning their spoken comments indicated that they were integrating the experience into their picture-making. Jeremy stood at a painting easel and making a vertical brown stroke with his brush announced: 'This is a tree,' then added as an afterthought, 'but it is going to be a snowball.'

Jeremy then proceeded to place some daubs of white paint on the branches he had painted, commenting: 'There, I've put some snow,' as he exchanged the white paint for brown in order to paint more branches.

Later, returning to the jar of white paint he discovered a lump in it and picking it up on the top of his brush he dabbed it on the paper. The lump of white paint fell to the floor, so Jeremy picked it up and pressed it to the paper with his fingers, spreading it over the surface as it yielded to his pressure. 'Look, I've made some snow,' he exclaimed excitedly to no one in particular.

His companion, Maurice, a very intelligent boy, chose to make a picture with crayons and with a touch of humorous imagination drew a child with a red umbrella on which fell red snow. 'Whoever saw red snow?' he muttered to himself. 'Now I'll have to do red snow on the ground as it's falling down red. Ha, ha, how funny, red snow, whoever saw red snow!'

Maurice was in no doubt of the difference between his flight of fancy and reality.

Sir Percy Nunn tells us that '. . . the soul of art like that of play is the joyous exercise of spontaneity'.[1] Five year old Gordon reflected the truth of this statement as one morning he let his imagination have full rein in his painting. After painting a sun in his picture he announced to me that he was going to give the sun some baby suns and he would paint them nearby 'because they wouldn't want to be far away from their Mummy'. Yet, only a few weeks later, this same child expressed scientific deductions in a painting of trees in his garden. He commented:

This is going to be an apple tree but it is only going to be green, nothing else because it is not apple time; it is the time when the little buds are right inside. There is another tree a bit further down the garden, it is an acorn tree. It does look like that down the end of the garden, doesn't it? Because it is far away, it looks littler, doesn't it?

Sometimes a knowledge of circumstances makes it possible to discern how a child tries to penetrate the mysteries of a puzzling

[1] Nunn, Percy, *Education: Its Data and First Principles*, Arnold 1925, p. 88.

experience through drawing. Five year old Marion's pictures during the year which followed the death of her baby sister often included direct or indirect references to the incident. Her commentary gives a glimpse of the nature of the process.

I'm going to put Jesus' home in the sky. A roof, a chimney pot, the next pot is going to be blue. Now a green chimney pot. . . . That is the door of Jesus' garage. A blue door. Now some windows in his house, that's all. Oh, no, here's Catherine up in the sky. Catherine is Jesus' little girl. I'll colour her hat red. Some eyes for her, too. I'll give her red eyes. Her skirt is yellow. Blue hands she has. Brown legs, green shoes.

Marion serves also to illustrate Ruth Griffiths' observation that a child may form '. . . certain childish theories of his own to explain things to himself, much as primitive man invented theories (now extant in myths) to explain the mysteries of the universe'.[1] She had obviously been told that Jesus lived in 'the bright blue sky'. Being puzzled as to how he remained in space she provided her own solution by placing him on a spring:

This is supposed to be your home, where you will be at half term, Miss M. . . . You have got a proper house with a bathroom in it, haven't you? Have you got a little girl? I thought you had not. You have got us, though. Mummy has me and I've got my dolls. This is you taking a photograph of your house. You have put on your pretty frock with blue spots on it. This is Jesus. He lives in heaven and I think he must go up on a spring. I am going to do Catherine in this picture. You know she is my baby sister who died, so she lives with Jesus, you see. She had better be on a spring, too, hadn't she?

Other children indicated in pictorial form their interpretation of ideas gained through instruction, such as Bible stories. Though their pictures may bear the influence of illustrations shown to the children they also frequently reveal the way in which a child tries to weave new experiences into a known pattern. Miles, aged six, having returned from a seaside holiday, drew a picture of a beach with a Blackpool Tower in the background, telling his teacher: 'This is Jesus talking to the people on the sand at Blackpool.' The five year old in the conversation below showed how he, too, related the life of baby Jesus to his own experiences:

[1] *A Study of Imagination in Early Childhood*, p. 309.

Teacher   Tell me about your picture.
Basil   That's the baby Jesus.
Teacher   I suppose the other person is Mary.
Basil   Oh no, that's the baby-sitter. His mother has gone out with God.

Sometimes a young child may reflect sensitivity in spontaneous paintings concerning Jesus like those done by two seven year olds: Yvonne conveyed the friendliness of Jesus in her painting of 'children bringing flowers to Jesus'; Paul expressed a feeling of compassion in a picture of 'Jesus healing the blind man'. More rarely do young children spontaneously portray God, but when they make such an attempt the Deity is likely to be given human physical characteristics and pictured as being in the sky regions. This can be seen in six year old Andrew's picture of God in the sky overlooking a red bus, drawn shortly after some impromptu discussion about God had taken place among a group of children in his class.[1] Seven year old Angela's picture of 'God outside his shop where he keeps all the food and clothes he gives us' suggests that this is her interpretation of God as 'Giver'.

(c) *Recording of words*

Children come to a realization that writing may serve a similar function to the spoken word as a means of communicating facts, feelings and ideas.

The initial interest in writing is usually shown by countless requests to the adult. Six year old Hazel's simply dictates: *'Please write:* This is my house. The boy and girl are in the garden.' Jennifer's describes a mood: *'You write:* The lady is happy because she is going to a party.' From such beginnings children will proceed to experiment in the art of recording words, which may be accompanied by pictures, as was Jane's account of her weekend activities.

I went to see if one of my mums friends had had her baby but she hadn't. So I told my mum she hadn't had her baby. On Saturday I went to . . . Fete I had a ride on the ponys and I saw the Royal Marines, then I had a go on the ping pong balls but I never wond anything.

Derek, an intelligent seven year old, was content with the written word alone. As a result of looking at an encyclopaedia in school he

[1] See back cover.

carried out some experiments, after which he presented his teacher with the following spontaneous written record of his findings.

If I put a heavy weght in warter it would sink. And if I put a weght in a cup of warter the warter would rise because the warter would not have any room. If you were doing the washing up and you put all the cups and saucers and the plates in the warter would rise because warter would not have space.

Margaret of the same age also presented her knowledge of the sequence of human life without aid of pictures when she wrote about

How you grow

When you or any other child were yong and used to go in a pram and lern to walk and talk now you can hear about how you used to lern to walk and talk like any other child. Now when you were born you would cry and scream when anything was done to you if not that you would be sleeping. When you are biger you go in a push-chair when you get evan bigger you are let out of your pushchair and lern to walk. Soon you have lernt to talk and you get on very well. Of corse you have raeins and when you're about three or four years old you can Walk Without your raeins Soon you go to school from class to class you get to the top one day then in another school. When you've been in three schools you go to College or to work in a shop or office Soon you get mairred and live in a new house Soon you've got settled down in your new house then you want a baby you lie in bed waiting hoping your baby will come soon then one unexpekting day it comes then the story starts over again how it was told each time when there is a baby.

Sharon, a very lively six year old, when writing her story of the Dragon family entered into the realms of imagination both in her words and in the illustrations which accompanied them.

Once upon a time there was a dragon it was red with blue and green spots He did not live by himself He had a wife Mrs Dragon Mrs Dragon said to Mr Dragon I think I am having a child Mr Dragon said I will go to the horspital Next day they went to the horspital. Mrs Dragon did have a child Mr Dragon was proud. The babys name was Chick.

As with stories expressed orally (p. 36), children sometimes concentrate on a theme in a series of written stories. Sharon's tale of 'The Spotted Dragon' was one of a number she wrote when she seemed to be working over impressions regarding the relationship of the sexes. Here is another one:

> Once upon a time there was a tigu (tiger)
> the tigu said I am lonli
> I have no wif said tigu
> I have no home said tigu
> I will go and find a wif
> so tigu went to find a wif
> He met a tigu
> Oh tigu will you marry me
> the tigu said oh yes plees but I am a ladi
> that dusnt matu (matter) I am a man
> so the tigus marryid

There are times when the essence of poetry seems inherent in the simplicity and spontaneity of young children's writing. Such qualities are in the record of a visit to the sea and a description of dreaming written by seven year old Joanna and Linda.

> One day I went a skipping to the sea
> I played in the sand with my dog
> He found a shell
> Inside the shell there was a fish
>
> *Joanna*

> I saw as I was a walking
> I was having a dream
> The most wondflest of all
> I did not awake
> I did not asleep
> But I went on with my think
>
> *Linda*

It must be emphasized that these children had been allowed time to grow in their experience of words. Their teacher would have perceived the seed of later written expression in four year old Joy's haphazard incidental play with words, as sitting on the top of a climbing frame, swinging a balloon to and fro, she sang quietly and rhythmically to herself

If the wind came along,
Swing along,
Swing along,
Swing along;

If the wind came along,
Swing along,
Swing along,
Swing along,

Da dee, da dee, da dee dee,
Jingle bells, jingle bells,
How are you today.

To summarize

Younger children, then, seek for meaning by questioning both adults and one another. Their queries often arise from their physical exploration of the world about them, which, in turn, leads them to constructive experiment and a deepening of understanding. Meanwhile, as their circle of human contact widens, they develop ideas of self and try to enter into the role of other people through imitation. In their spontaneous activities and their relationships with others they reveal the intensity of their emotional life and their mode of thinking. Gradually, the expression of ideas gained from these experiences, whether through speech, art or the written word, becomes increasingly comprehensible, not only to the children themselves, but to others. Many of these experiences come through play, bearing out the truth of Froebel's assertion that 'Play is not trivial, it is highly serious and of the deepest significance'.

2 *The Junior School Years*

Discovery through spoken questions

IN ADDITION TO keeping records of children's spontaneous questions, contributed by parents and teachers, more direct methods were used in obtaining the material presented in this section, including shorthand summaries of conversations I had with groups of children. The children concerned represent widely different social and educational backgrounds, and a development from the egocentric tendency noticeable in the younger children's thought towards a growing awareness of other people's points of view can be discerned.[1] Some of the parents interviewed reported a reduction in the number of questions asked of them during this period, whilst others mentioned an increase in children's reference to books, especially encylopaedias, and the stimulation of children's curiosity by television programmes. The less frequent questions to parents may have been due to several reasons. In some instances it seemed likely that the children recognized parents' limitations. It must also be remembered that during these years they grow in their ability to discover answers from books, since they have usually acquired considerable reading skill. Furthermore, junior children also ask questions of each other as well as of adults outside the home.

The main topics covered by the questions asked of parents and teachers concerned objects in the environment, the universe, animals and plants, human beings (including origin, destiny and behaviour) and religion. There were, however, fewer spontaneous and specific questions about the last topic: the majority of questions of a religious nature were oblique and concerned such matters as creation

[1] See Piaget, Jean, *The Psychology of Intelligence*, Part III, Routledge and Kegan Paul 1950.

and human behaviour. The questions below represent a cross-section of the enquiries.

Objects in the environment

However do they fit the tiny bits of machinery into little watches?
How are dictionaries made?
How does a zip work?
How does a violin make music?
When you pull the string in the bedroom the light goes on, and then when you pull it again it goes off. However does it work?
How does a nail stay in wood?
How is it that planes can fly in the air without falling down?
At home we have a basket-work stool which creaks when you are not sitting on it. Why?
Why does the reflection in a spoon go a queer shape?
Why do eggs turn spoons brown?

Universe, plants, animals

How do colours of sunrise and sunset get into the sky?
Why do some cliffs crumble away?
Why are there differences in colour in forget-me-not flowers on the same stalk?
What was the first kind of animal in the world?
How far away is the sun?
How did the plants get their names?
Why is it that some animals breathe much more quickly than we do?
When you get seeds in a packet they are so small. How do they grow into something as big as a cabbage?
What causes thunder and lightning?
Why is sea salty?
How do tides happen?
If the earth is a tremendous magnet, how is it that it doesn't make the point of the compass turn downwards?
Is it summer all the year round at the equator?
If things weigh heavier on earth and less on the moon, it must be because of the amount of gravity plus the consistency of the object, mustn't it? Why is an object weightless in space then?
If the moon is a chip off the sun like the earth, why should the moon not have an atmosphere like the earth?
Is the world flat at the poles because God made it before he had a pair of compasses?
How do mummy hedgehogs grow baby hedgehogs inside? However are they born with all the prickles sticking out?

Human beings

When you turn round and round why does it make you feel dizzy?
When you bend your little finger down why does the next one come down too?
If you say your cousin is 'once removed' from you, whatever does it mean?
When you are married you can have babies. Can you have them when you are not married?
Why do you jump when you get a shock?
How do we grow?
On T.V. there was a man eating glass, why didn't it cut him?
Why do people make things that are not good for you?
What happens to your veins when you grow taller? Do they just stretch thinner?

Religion

What is the Holy Ghost?
You told us that we can only be sure that the story of Robin Hood is partly true. How then can you be sure that the story of Jesus is absolutely true?
Who first thought of putting all the saints' letters into a book called the Bible?
Jesus was a Jew, why don't Jewish people believe in him?
When we say our prayers why do we close our eyes and put our hands together?
How many years did Jesus live?
What is the difference between the Jewish religion, the Roman Catholic and Chapel?

Miscellaneous

Why do we say 'touch wood'?
Who invented punctuation marks?
What is the origin of April Fool's day?
How did people first think of north, south, east, west?

Conversations with Children

In spite of disadvantages inherent in a more direct approach, where an adult provides some stimulus, the material obtained from these conversations seems worth noting. It will be seen, for instance, that allowing for the degree of control inevitably imposed by discussion technique on the children's trend of thought, the queries put forward by the forty boys and girls concerned were widely varied, ranging from the type of question asked by the younger children about everyday affairs (How are matches made?) to those involving thought-provoking moral issues (Is it right to kill someone if he has killed someone else?).

A. *Eight and nine year olds*

Records of two discussions between children of eight and nine years of age illustrate their curiosity and speculative attempts to solve problems. They also show that in some ways they continue to operate as the younger children. There is again evidence of an interest in the puzzling aspects of the everyday world. (How do they make fridges cold?) The attempt to reconcile new information with previous ideas is again seen in Audrey's speculative thought concerning the habitat of the dead and Guy's query about the reasons why the men in rockets did not see God. There are, however, important developments as interests expand and questioning becomes more precise. Enquiry extends during this period to matters concerning space and time, seen in the queries: What was it like to be a caveman? What would it be like to live on the moon? Many of the questions related to the universe, and causes and origins were sought. (How does petrol make a car go? How was God made first?) There was also more frequent expression of doubt, as for example Keith's query about the possibility of God creating the world in seven days.

Conversations with the eight and nine year olds were prefaced by the reading of an extract from the account of the Mad Hatter's Tea Party from *Alice in Wonderland*, after which the children were presented with the query: Supposing Alice had been invited to a clever tea-party attended by very wise people, what questions do you think she would have asked?

> *George*   You know the shapes of stars? Well, how do they get the lines making them into animals and things?
> (Further questioning indicated that George had seen illustrations of signs of the Zodiac. He was puzzled because he could not see lines joining star to star in the sky. The other children cleared up the mystery for him.)
>
> *Guy*   It would cost a lot to study the stars, wouldn't it? You would have to have a very large telescope. I think bits of the sun come off and turn into stars.

George	Well, I think the earth is a bit of sun come off and it has cooled off. . . . told us that. It is still hot in the middle of the world where it has not cooled off.
Guy	How do they build buildings, like churches? How do they join doors on to the bricks? They can't use nails can they, because they wouldn't go into the bricks?
George	How does petrol make a car go?
James	A thing that puzzles me is how guitars and other instruments make sounds like they do. How is sound made?
Guy	How do they make electricity?
Miss M.	Perhaps you have some idea?
Guy	I think they might put it into a big round thing and send it through pipes.
Geoffrey	Do they find electricity on the ground and put it into wire? They might burn coal and get it from that.
Bryan	Perhaps they put coal into some liquid and electricity comes from it?
Sheila	How do they manage to make charcoal out of coal?
Lynn	They don't, they make it out of sticks.
Audrey	Just how is rain made?
George	It comes up like sea and gets collected up in the clouds.
Lesley	The clouds go behind a hill and fetch water from the sea.
Audrey	How do they make fridges cold?
Brenda	When they made the first coal-mine, how did they manage to dig down all that way?
Guy	You know George was talking about the earth just now. Some people say God made the world, but I'm not sure about that.
George	Well, I think it just came off the sun.
Sheila	I'd like to know who made people?
George	Now that's a question: who made people? Who started it all? Anyway, how was God made first to make the world?
Guy	They say God lives in the sky, so when the rockets go up, why don't the men see him?
Audrey	When people die and go into graves what happens to them? They say their souls go up in the sky.
Miss M.	What do you think about it?
Audrey	Maybe they live near the sun when they die and no one çan go near the sun because it is too hot, so they don't see them.
Bryan	Are there any more worlds where people live?

A group of nine year olds, together with ten year old James, were engaged in a similar discussion.

Susan	I'd like to know how many planets there are.
Keith	How are the stars made? They might be little bits of things broken off the sun.
James	What would it be like to live on the moon?
Simon	It would be interesting to know what it was like to be a caveman.

(There was a pause here in the contributions and I directed the children's thoughts.)

Miss M.	There might be things puzzling Alice about God?
Simon	Yes, like just how he made men?
Susan	How did Jesus make people better, like making blind people see? I'd like to know how God made the world, too.
James	And who made the seeds to make the trees?
Keith	How did God manage to make the world in seven days?
Simon	He didn't. Just because you have read it in some book doesn't mean it is true. I don't know the answer though. Miss . . . said God made it in two weeks, I think.

Then followed a spate of questions, among them :

Just how does God make seeds turn into wood?
How did he make the days?
How did he name the days and months?
How did he make the sun begin?
How was the sky made?
How does God make the wind?

Susan	Now, I read in a book that the wind is made by a cloud with a face on it.
Miss M.	Did you believe that was true?
Susan	No, I didn't.
Miss M.	What do you believe?
Susan	I really don't know.
Simon	Oh, I do. It is God blowing.
James	It is when a cloud bursts and air comes out, perhaps.
Keith	Is it the world travelling round right fast?
Simon	Can't be, 'cos then there would be wind all the time, everywhere, and there isn't.
James	If the world stopped going round, would the people in Australia fall off?

Wendy   What would have happened if Jesus was never born. And another thing, why is it different times in different countries? I can't puzzle it out at all.

B. *Ten and eleven year olds*

A study of conversations with ten and eleven year old children gives some indication of their interests and the nature of their speculative thought. The first discussion took place after a group of boys had been listening to a BBC Junior Science programme, when it was suggested that they might imagine that someone from the BBC asked them what questions they would like answered:

Martin   How does the tropical wood of millions of years ago change into coal? I know forests turned to coal, but not how.

Leslie   I'd ask just how they make rockets.

Miss M.   What made you think of that question?

Leslie   I heard a serial on the wireless and it was about rockets and the future.

Richard   Is it possible to make life out of chemicals?

Miss M.   Did something make you think about this?

Richard   Yes, I've seen a TV programme on Tuesday evenings. It was called Andromeda. They received messages from outer space, and made things live. They made a woman. Now I wonder if a human can make things live. I'd like to know if a baby could be made from chemicals. I mean without being made in the ordinary way babies come from mothers and fathers.

Carl   I'd like to know how to keep animals alive. When we went camping with the school last year, lots of rabbits were dying. They put stuff down at the farm. It seems cruel.

Miss M.   Have you a pet, Carl?

Carl   Yes, I've got a dog, and a budgie and once I got fifty mice. I'm going to get more soon. I gave the fifty away, 'cos Mum said they was too many about the place. I don't like animals dying, though. I don't want my dog to die, that's why I ask the question.

Paul   How do they teach the chimpanzees to do the tricks they do in a circus?

Miss M.   What made you think of that question, Paul?

Paul   Well, yesterday I heard that they had sent a monkey into space. I wondered how they taught the monkey to pull the levers to come back to earth.

(This statement provoked much speculative discussion and only a partial recording was possible.)

Richard I think there is someone who shows the monkey what to do. They keep on showing the monkey how to do it until the monkey imitates them. Do you think they are monkeys with especially good brains?

Jonathan Perhaps the monkey has a bit of human life in him, like Richard was talking about just now.

Martin I think they have different colour lights.

Peter Yes, I think I know what you mean. The monkey would be attracted to the lights because there would be food there.

Leslie The food might be plastic food.

Richard Yes, and he would pull a lever to get the food.

Andrew What is the difference between human and animal blood?

(A pause occurred at this point and I directed the children's thoughts.)

Miss M. Have you ever had questions come into your mind about God?

(The instant reaction to this query was a very spontaneous, 'Yes'.)

Richard Could it be possible that there is no God because it might be that someone made up what is in the Bible?

Martin Well, I wonder if there is such a person as God. If there is, why ever doesn't he show himself?

Leslie And another thing, if God made everything, I wonder and wonder and wonder how God made himself?

Andrew How do we really know Jesus lived on this earth?

Jonathan My question is like Leslie's, if God made us, who made God?

Carl However did God get Jesus to do all those miracles? I've often wondered if the stars are made of some kind of chemical.

Peter Yes, they might be. And if God made the stars, I wonder how he made them. I don't know the answer to that one, but I would like to.

At the request of these boys another discussion was arranged and this was prefaced by suggesting to the children that the BBC had announced that they were arranging a new programme to be called Children's Question Box. Children were invited to send in questions of any kind, the BBC promising to get the wisest people they knew to answer the questions. The following is an outline of the discussion which ensued.

Martin   How did the word ten come into the world?

Miss M.   What made you think of that question?

Martin   Well, I have often wondered why ten is ten. It could have been another word for ten, couldn't it? Why did it happen to be ten?

Jonathan   When will the decimal coinage come to this country? Most other countries have decimal coinage and we might get into the Common Market if we had it.

Miss M.   Would you say it would be a good idea?

Jonathan   Oh yes, because it is easier, because you just work in tens.

Andrew   If all the rivers in Great Britain were put together how long would they stretch?

Leslie   How deep is the Niagara Falls?

Jonathan   How did God create man?

Martin   It might have been a machine he used.

Miss M.   What do you think of such an idea?

Martin   Well, machines do lots of things these days, so it might be possible.

Leslie   Why do we kill lambs?

Miss M.   Was there a special reason for your question, Leslie?

Leslie   I've heard about these vegetarians going around. Mind you I like meat myself, but I like to see lambs in the fields, too. It does seem a bit cruel when you think about it.

Paul   I've got a different kind of question. When they build a big building like the Empire State building how does it keep up?

Martin   How are mountains formed?

Richard   Probably something like this. There is some radio pressure coming up in the earth and the radio force comes up in the middle and some kind of force pushes up and squeezes so that a mound comes up.

David   I would like to know how long has Mount Everest been in existence.

Jonathan   It would be interesting to know how men found out how to build bridges.

Richard   Perhaps they used scaffolding.

David   I should think they made a bell-shaped thing that floated with men in it.

Andrew They must have dived down and put scaffolding up somehow. What about the Romans, they didn't have diving things, did they?

David   Why did cannibals eat human beings?

Richard They couldn't find any animals to eat, I expect. Maybe someone shot someone and he fell on the fire and a dog started to eat—perhaps an arm—and so men thought it might taste good and they tried it. We don't do it now, though.

Miss M. Why do you think we don't do it now?

Martin Well, we are civilized and we think it is cruel and anyway it is against the law now.

Jonathan I'd like to know a lot more about animals. Why do kangaroos jump so far?

Martin How many tributaries are there into the River Amazon?

Miss M. Why do you want to know?

Martin Well, people say different things. My auntie, she told me two hundred, and someone else I asked said one hundred and fifty.

Jonathan Talking about rivers and things, how is a delta formed?

Leslie A good question would be, was it a good thing to change over to buses from trams?

Miss M. What do you think?

Leslie Well during fogs trams are better, I think, because they go on lines and people can get home from the factories more easily.

At this point the children were asked to suppose that the BBC decided to put on a question-box programme for children about religion. This evoked the following suggestions:

Martin How many miracles did Jesus perform?

Miss M. What made you interested in that question?

Martin We keep on hearing the same one, like the feeding of the five thousand. Sometimes when they begin you think it is a new one, but it always turns out one you've heard before. I would like to know if there are any more. I should think there might be. I'm tired of hearing the same stories.

Donald How do we know when the world is coming to an end? Our Vicar said that Jesus will visit us when the world comes to an end. How shall we know when that's going to happen? How does the Vicar know Jesus may come, anyhow?

Jonathan	How many religious laws are there?
Miss M.	What do you mean by a religious law?
Jonathan	Like you should pray to God every day. You shouldn't work on the Sabbath and things like that.
Leslie	About those songs in the *Songs of Praise*. Nowadays they are changing over all the hymns and I'd like to know if the hymns in the old *Songs of Praise* have any connection with the songs of nowadays, like Cliff Richards sings.
Anthony	How prayer started? That would be interesting. When Jesus came into the world they knew Our Father, but I would like to know how did they make words up to fit into a prayer first of all. How did they think of praying?
Richard	I expect it was to ask for mercy when they had done a sin. When they were in prison some of them sang and prayed sometimes, like Paul. They think they are talking to God and no one else but God can hear them.
Mark	Praying is asking for remission of sins to God.
Miss M.	What do you mean?
Mark	Wrong doings?
Donald	When we pray how do we know we really are talking to God because we might just be talking to ourselves?
Paul	If God and Jesus are real people why don't they show themselves on this earth?
Richard	How do we know that the stories about Jesus are not just a fable because the Greeks had gods and made up stories about them and they were not true gods?
Mark	Why doesn't the Holy Ghost come down looking like he is instead of looking like a dove?
Jonathan	Did Ben Hur really exist?
Andrew	If there was such a person as Jesus, why don't we know a lot about him? We only know about his birth and he was twelve and when he did some miracles.
Leslie	How great was Samson's strength?
Paul	Is it true that Moses went up into the mountain and found the Ten Commandments?
Mark	How do they know Mars is real and there is life on it? I saw a serial on TV and it showed life on the planets. I wondered if it was really true or if they were making it up.
Jonathan	How did the ancient gods like Thor disappear when the people believed in the one true God?

Mark   Is it right if a man kills someone, to kill him?
Miss M. What do you think?
Mark   I don't think it is right because then you lose two lives.
Jonathan Why in olden times did they burn a man's hand and send
         him home and then in a week or a month later if his
         hand had not healed they used to kill him? I think it is
         wrong, they should have a trial in court and put his hand
         on a Bible.

Even though there was some measure of adult control of these
conversations they yielded a variety of spontaneous queries and
comments. An interest in 'science', fanned by television and wireless
programmes was very apparent, and it was noted that some children,
like Mark, were in the process of working over whether the ideas put
forward on television programmes were feasible. The boys were
very ready to enter into speculative thought as indicated in the comments about the chimpanzees in space. Martin's comment that God
may have made man by using a machine was accepted as a serious
proposition by the other members of the group. The boys were also
avid collectors of facts, often mentioning encyclopaedias as sources
of information, and time, space and primary causes were frequently
involved in their queries.

There was no doubt about the boys' interest in religious matters:
their questions voiced curiosity, doubts, bewilderment and occa-
sional concern over moral issues. Though they seemed very bored
by over-familiar material they were nevertheless most anxious to
have an opportunity to talk over problems that were puzzling them.
There was evidence that scientific and religious concepts were
coming into conflict with one another, though it was interesting that
scientific as well as religious conceptions were being challenged. An
example of this was Mark's query: How do they know Mars is
real and there is life on it?

The next two records of discussions concern a group of seven
girls, aged ten and eleven years. The BBC Junior Science programme again served as an opening, but the girls were rather half-
hearted about their enjoyment of these programmes. When they, like
the boys, were invited to put forward questions for such a programme, the following comments and queries were made:

Mary   What is it in the chemicals that makes those things grow
        in water-glass?

(This query referred to an experiment carried out in the class-room.)

> *Pamela* I would like to know where they cook our school dinners now?

(This question arose as the dinners were being sent from a new kitchen. The query was answered by other children.)

> *June* Where do the germs that make your teeth decay come from? Do they come from the food you eat?
> *Penelope* I've been wondering since you let us have the magnets and the iron filings, just *what* it was that made them stick to the magnets?
> *Mary* How do they make leather?
> *Claire* What about glass? How do they make glass?
> *June* If a plant comes from a seed, where did that seed come from?
> *Desney* Why do sea urchins have spikes?
> *Claire* To protect them, of course.
> *Kathryn* Why do camels have two humps and dromedaries only one?
> *Mary* You know, that reminds me of another question I'd like answered. How did the zebra get his stripes?

(Here followed a great deal of discussion about mixed breeding.)

> *Mary* Talking of animals, I would like to ask why it is that kangaroos and koala bears are only in Australia?
> *June* Wouldn't it be interesting to know how people manage to make different glasses for different people's eyes?
> *Kathryn* They say the sun is a ball of fire. Is it true?
> *June* Well, they say God made the sun.
> *Miss M.* Have you ever had any puzzling thoughts about God?

(This query raised an instant spontaneous response.)

> *Desney* If God made the world, who made God?
> *Mary* I know the answer. God never had a beginning or an end. It is like the sky. If you built a wall in the sky it is never the end because there is always sky beyond it.
> *Claire* I've often wondered what the stars are made of and how did the sun and moon come to be.
> *June* If God is a spirit you don't really know where he is because he might be behind a cloud. You don't know he is really there if you cannot see him.

Kathryn   Everyone talks as though God is a man. How do they know he isn't a woman?

Claire   He might have some children.

Desney   Well, I want to know how do you know he is a man?

Mary   It puzzled me how God can be in one part of the world, like being here, and being in Africa at the same time.

These girls were very eager for further sessions, and on the second occasion they needed no introduction, for they had their questions ready. They were allowed to put these forward, after which their thoughts were directed into questions concerning religion.

June   Why don't the stars fall down?

Penelope   How did the stars begin? Did they begin by sparks from the sun?

Kathryn   Why don't the stars show in the day-time? The sun does, but the stars don't, do they? Just how did all the planets get into the sky?

Claire   God made them.

Penelope   But *how* did he make them? How is it that human beings can stay up in the air in space and we can't when we're on earth?

June   Just what is gravity? I don't understand it.

Mary   Why do we go on believing in Father Christmas coming on sledges and so on? He ought to come on a bus these days.

(Here followed a discussion about St Nicholas and how young children believe in Father Christmas and most of us like to pretend to believe in him long after we know the truth, etc.)

Claire   Why can rockets go further into the air than aeroplanes?

Kathryn   Rockets have got special equipment that aeroplanes have not got.

Celia   Why is it colder the higher up you go because you would think it would get hotter as you get nearer the sun?

Desney   Is the sun really a ball of fire?

June   What are the things that look like eyes, nose and mouth on the moon?

Penelope   Why is it we can use chalk on a blackboard but we cannot use wax crayons?

June   Why do we make missiles to blow each other up? Why can't we have peace? It's so silly to blow each other up. There *must* be some way?

Claire   Why doesn't the sun get cold? What keeps it hot?

Mary   How do we get cotton? Does the cotton seed come from a plant or what?

Desney   Yes, and how does cotton actually form from the seed?

Mary   Why is it that only ladies have children when they are married and gentlemen don't?

As the flow of questions slowed up at this point, it was suggested to the children that they might imagine that the BBC informed us that they were arranging a programme about religion for children. The suggestion brought forth a response of groans. The girls found some difficulty in expressing their reasons for their dislike. This appeared to be due to a sense of guilt because they had dared to suggest that religion might be uninteresting. Further comment also indicated that they anticipated it would be boring, since it would mean a repetition of what they had heard previously.

Miss M.   Perhaps the BBC knew this and they wanted to arrange a programme which would interest children, so they asked us to give them questions which we would like answered?

June   Why do the priests go to the church wearing all black things and their white collars?

Mary   When Jesus was born could God have known they couldn't get into the inn?

Claire   He made it like that, I think.

Desney   Why do nuns have to have their hair chopped off?

June   Clipped off would be a better word, or shaved?

Claire   Why is it nuns can't speak to each other? Someone told me they were allowed to talk to each other only for three years? Is that true?

Kathryn   And another thing, why can't nuns marry?

Mary   Why do people have different languages? Is it because God made it like that?

Penelope   I know the answer to that. Once all people spoke the same language, and then they quarrelled so God stopped them and made them speak all different languages.

Desney   Why are people made different colours?

Kathryn   Is it the sun in Africa that makes them brown?

Mary   But people are born brown in this country and we haven't much sun, so that can't be the answer.

The girls' questions covered a variety of topics, ranging from the everyday question: Where are our school dinners cooked? to the profound enquiry: Why do we make missiles to blow each other up? They shared the boys' interest in the universe and origins and were also concerned about human relationships. They, too, were more than ready to discuss religious matters when they realized that the atmosphere was sympathetic and permissive. They seemed to experience relief in feeling that their views were respected and welcomed the chance to express doubts and bewilderment. After each discussion period, as we walked to the school from the hall where the discussions had taken place, both boys and girls eagerly followed up points raised in discussion and made repeated requests for further opportunities for question and discussion.

Discovery of the world around

The questions asked by the over-sevens included those seeking information about objects in the environment. Here a comparison of the young children's reactions to magnets (p. 22) with that of a group of ten year old girls is interesting, since it illustrates both similarities and developments. The girls, like the younger children, had had little previous experience with magnets and their pre-liminary response was almost identical in that they were very excited and made indiscriminate investigations. But this phase passed quickly as they of their own accord introduced some selective and purposeful activity into their experiments. They decided to divide the articles into those which were attracted by magnets and those which were not. They tried out quite elaborate experiments like that of using the magnetic force as a principle underlying the use of magnets in a 'building' operation, a procedure which called for considerable skill and control. The fact that a penny failed to adhere to the magnet caused one girl to spend some time in a fruitless, yet patient, investigation of the possibilities of extra pressure. The question 'Why won't it?' was expressed and was raised at a later discussion when these girls were talking about questions they would like answered. They were also very quick to see analogies: the reaction of articles attracted to the magnet, for instance, reminded one girl of a 'crane' and another of the 'twist'.

These same children when discussing the BBC Junior Science programme had mentioned the fact that they preferred the pro-grammes when there was 'something to do' even if it merely entailed watching the teacher carrying out an experiment while the

programme was in progress. When asked if they carried out some of
the experiments which were suggested, their replies indicated that
they lost heart because they so often found that the necessary
materials and equipment were not available at home.

Rousseau was aware of this innate desire and need of children
actually to experience discovery of natural forces, and the way in
which Emile's knowledge of magnetism developed through access
to materials in the company of a sympathetic adult is worth quoting.
Rousseau describes how Emile's interest in magnetism was first
aroused through the observation :

> . . . that different bodies such as amber, glass and wax, when
> rubbed, attract straws, and that others do not attract them. By
> accident we discovered one that has a virtue more extraordinary
> still—that of attracting at a distance, and without being rubbed,
> iron filings and other bits of iron. This peculiarity amused us for
> some time before we saw any use in it. At last we found out that
> it may be communicated to iron itself, when magnetized to a certain
> degree.[1]

Rousseau then relates how during a visit to a fair, Emile watched
a demonstration by a juggler in which wax ducks floating on water
were made to pursue a piece of bread. This, Emile, who had been
encouraged to look for causes, perceived to be due to magnetic
forces, and as a result he evolved a similar successful experiment
using a well magnetized needle enclosed in white wax. Having
made the discovery of the juggler's secret he returned to the fair to
demonstrate his knowledge of the trick. We then read of how the
astonished juggler invited the boy to return the next day, when,
although the juggler was successful in attracting the duck, to the
child's confusion . . . 'the duck made sport of him, by whirling
round and round as it swam about the edge of the basin'.[1]

The juggler finally revealed that a powerful magnet had been
moved by a child concealed beneath the table. Rousseau then
describes how :

> Having learned that a magnet acts through other bodies, we were
> all impatience until we had made an apparatus like the one we had
> seen—a hollow table-top with a very shallow basin adjusted upon it
> and filled with water, a duck rather more carefully made, and so on.

[1] Rousseau, *Emile*. Extracts translated by Eleanor Worthington, D. C.
Heath, Boston 1899, pp. 133-138.

Watching this apparatus attentively and often, we finally observed that the duck, when at rest, nearly always turned in the same direction. Following up the experiment by examining this direction, we found it to be from south to north. Nothing more was necessary; our compass was invented, or might as well have been. We had begun to study physics.[1]

Rousseau also realized the peculiar demands and excitement awaiting children in the outdoor world, the truth of which is contained in Leslie Paul's account of the challenge he and other town children encountered in the countryside.

We came out of our suburbs into this country as into another land. No streets ran straightly, dully, here. No rows of windows staring down at us with grandmotherly eyes. Here everything was new. The hedge and trees lived for themselves according to their own laws, which were not our laws. Nature clutched its secrets to itself and we had to prize out our discoveries, rats and voles in the ditches, birds nesting in thickets, insects crepitating in the grass. The meadows and woods and lanes led, not to dull safe places, but to undiscovered lands. It was all so uncharted and so endless in its variety. We had to make maps in our heads. We never knew what we might find. And we ourselves, we were free in it.[2]

A similar joy of discovery seems reflected in eight year old Jennifer's simple account of her country experience.

I like to go in the field to play at things, speshelly looking for berry's and wineflowers. they are white prickely things. I have to put my gluvs on. in the summer there is buttercups and dases. all sots. I like doing thees things better than playing ordanery things like hide and seek and other games.

Jennifer told me how much she looked forward to the time when she would be permitted to join the annual school camping expedition, having caught the enthusiasm of the older children recently returned. One of Jennifer's classmates joined in the conversation and told me that his favourite spot in the country was a stream where he could sail his boat, a boyhood joy shared by John Masefield in his recollection of 'mud-larks'.

[1] Rousseau, *Emile*, pp. 133-138.
[2] Paul, Leslie, *The Living Hedge*, Faber and Faber 1946, p. 18.

Sometimes I was taken on a mud-lark up the mill-stream, dressed for the occasion in my oldest clothes and strongest boots. Passing under the viaduct, I came to that water, as it ran through a pasture turned up into red heaps by multitudinous moles. Here, for hours, one could sail home-made boats down the stream, prodding them with sticks when they stuck, and getting filthy and happy beyond easy description.

At the end of mud-larks, when all the ships had been sunk, or had gone downstream out of reach, we walked home happy and filthy, perhaps modelling the wet red clay into the images of birds' nests with eggs inside them, for that clay incites all children to be potters.[1]

Such outdoor pursuits, so popular with junior children, bring them into personal encounter with natural forces, whose laws have to be respected. This encounter may include the control of man-made objects, as was the case with nine year old Peter. He told me, with great zest, how he enjoyed riding his bicycle '. . . because I like speed. I see how fast I can go uphill. That's smashing. It's right hard though when there's a gale blowing.' Philip of nine years, who invited me to join him in sailing his yacht on the park lake, revealed that he had faced a similar problem, for he explained: 'You have to know which way the wind is blowing to set your sail.' James, a year older, seemed to be trying to express the same exhilarating sense gained by wrestling with water, this time in the throes of learning to swim.

My favrite thing of all is swimming. it is quit simple if you have enough courage. I can nearly do a length. I like swimming because it is a certain feeling about it and I think I am going to do a lot of swimming in my time

These boys in their personal discovery of natural forces shared feelings akin to those recalled by William Wordsworth.

> . . . at this hour
> The heart is almost mine with which I felt,
> From some hill-top on sunny afternoons,
> The paper kite high among fleecy clouds
> Pull at her rein like an impetuous courser;
> Or, from the meadows sent on gusty days,
> Beheld her breast the wind, then suddenly
> Dashed headlong, and rejected by the storm.[2]

[1] Masefield, John, *So Long to Learn*, Heinemann 1952, p. 8.
[2] Wordsworth, William, *The Prelude*, J. M. Dent 1940, Book 1, 491-498.

But although the period from eight to eleven years is one of boundless physical activity, especially for boys, there are quieter moments when some insight may come to a child, as it did to Leslie Paul in his recognition of a lark, hitherto only known through books. He remembers how his

> . . . eyes focused on a small creature climbing and fluttering in the air as though it were caught by a string. It was this that was singing, *this*! Of course, a lark? All my haphazard reading about birds acquired meaning. The insignificant morsel bursting with song was what the poets wrote about. It was real and actual too, unlike the many things one read of and never encountered in the suburban unicorn.[1]

From such experiences may arise moments when children may enter into that 'unconscious intercourse with beauty' when the realms of normal sensibility are transcended:

> Yes, I remember when the changeful earth
> And twice five summers on my mind had stamped
> The faces of the moving year, even then
> I held unconscious intercourse with beauty
> Old as creation, drinking in a pure
> Organic pleasure from the silver wreaths
> Of curling mist, or from the level plain
> Of waters coloured by impending clouds.[2]

Lest it should be thought that such moments come only to the more intelligent, let us consider Anthony Weaver's experience. He describes how excursions to the woods not only aroused the interest of children in Nature but disclosed an unsuspected sensitivity in duller children:

> I was often astonished to find a dull child who could hardly read and certainly not express himself in writing, startled at the sight of a view from a hill or the colour of flowers. He would paint a picture of this when the next opportunity offered and be eager to find out and tell the others more about it.[3]

---

[1] *The Living Hedge*, p. 11.
[2] Wordsworth, William, *The Prelude*, J. M. Dent 1940, Book 1, 559-566.
[3] Weaver, Anthony, *They Steal for Love*, Max Parrish 1959, p. 38.

Discovery through constructing

Like the younger children, the over-sevens may be stimulated to constructive effort as a result of exploring the properties of materials and objects. This fact has already been illustrated by the building operations executed by ten year old girls when experimenting with magnets (p. 59) and in John Masefield's reference to the 'home-made boats' and the clay which 'incites all children to be potters'.

Ten year old Stuart provided another example when in writing about what he liked doing best out of school hours he described the building of a dam:

> I like to go down to the stream with my friend Roger. The stream used to be clean when my Dad was young, but now it is dirty. The part where we go is very clear. We build a dam, and swing on the rope across the stream which we put up.
>
> We do this nearly every Sunday afternoon we sometimes do it Saturday afternoon. Sometimes we go all day Sunday, and take our lunch with us.
>
> To make a dam you get some large rocks, and make a wall across the stream. Get some strong sticks, and a stone and bang the sticks into the sandy bed. Fill the cracks in with mud and soil, but make sure they is no holes in.
>
> Why I like doing it is because sometimes in the Summer we sometimes go in our swimming trunks. To swim in the water where it is deep because the dam holds the water back. I like swinging from tree to tree on the rope. The stream is about 4 ft. broad.

Constructive activities which take place indoors may also involve considerable ingenuity. This may happen in schoolboy crazes, such as the popular paper aeroplanes and 'elastic pianos' mentioned in James Kenward's account of his own prep school life.

James Kenward first reports how he made a paper aeroplane 'capable of such aerobatics as looping the loop high up among the windows if weighted with exactly the right amount of changing-room soap'.[1] James equipped his aeroplanes with parachutes cut out of lavatory paper, each being about the size of a silver three-penny bit, partially folded, with a hole in the middle for balance. It was in the midst of playful experimenting with his invention that the boy became aware of the effect created by currents of hot air when one of his

[1] Kenward, James, *Prep School*, Penguin Books 1953, p. 48.

. . . parachutes drifted as though to land on the hot water pipes where the spectators were grouped warming their hands. But instead it went trembling up the wall to the ceiling, and there it stayed until a current edged it away from the support of the warm air and it landed on a desk. While it was yet in the air I dashed to the lavatory for the remainder of the toilet-roll. In the few minutes before the bell rang we manufactured hundreds of parachutes, and when the Assistant Master entered to begin the afternoon lesson all were safely launched and trembling against the ceiling, we being seated at our desks with our books open in front of us.[1]

The climax came as a boy opened the door sharply, whereupon

. . . the armada of parachutes, the paper snowfall, began to move away from its anchorage towards the centre of the room. Then it descended—upon books and inkpots, upon desks and table, upon the Assistant Master, and ourselves, all the more snowlike and mysterious for the hush that it created akin to the hush accompanying actual snow.[2]

But the Assistant Master did not appreciate the pedagogical possibilities inherent in his pupils' self-initiated activity, which might have formed an opportunity for the crystallizing of a few scientific principles! Though acknowledging the boys' ingenuity by the remark: 'I see—very ingenious', he gave a minus to everyone 'for laughing in class', the inventor of the parachutes being given two in addition for 'causing a breach of the peace'.

Kenward also relates how he and his companions invented an 'elastic piano' which 'originated with the twang of the paper pellet propelled elastically from between our teeth'.[3] This example shows how children will exert considerable effort to improve on their inventions, which may entail a laborious trial and error process. The first stage of development, which he calls 'the spinet stage', consisted of elastic (procured from inside discarded golf balls) wound increasingly tightly around a box to produce a musical sound. The final stage of the piano's evolution was due to an accidental discovery of a boy as he unwound the elastic from inside a golf ball under his desk lid during a lesson. In so doing he happened to pass the elastic over and under the body of his desk, and 'Nudged with his finger it produced a note of soft but splendid resonance.'[4] Thus the Elastic 'Grand' was invented.

[1] *Prep School*, p. 48   [2] Ibid., p. 49.   [3] Ibid., pp. 82-83.
[4] Ibid.

C

The boy James and his school fellows used considerable initiative and persistence both in acquiring the necessary materials for their constructive efforts and in evolving more refined models as a result of previous experiments. James Kenward does not tell of any repercussions which followed the purloining of the lavatory paper and soap. But the instance serves as a reminder of children's need to construct and how this may lead to impulsive acquisition of materials.

The way in which lack of materials may deter a child's urge to experiment and create was seen in the response to the science experiments suggested by the BBC. Ten year old Nancy also refers to a lack of materials when she writes of her delight in making dolls' clothes.

> I like making dolls cloths best in my spare time when I can get any cloth. Mostly I make them for my big doll for I find it easier.
> I make them mostly on either Saturday or Sunday. That is if I can find enough cloth. If I make my doll a play suit, I first of all cut out the materiall for the legs which I sew together. Then atatched to the breast, then with straps added I fasten on buttons and it is finished.
> I enjoy making cloths a great deal because I like thinking up new desiengs, and I am sure it will help if I make my own cloths later on.

Nancy in discussing her dressmaking experiments told how she made newspaper patterns 'because then you can make sure both sides are the same and get an idea of how it fits'. She also wished that she had got 'a proper pair of scissors' at home as the pair she was permitted to use 'jagged the material something awful'.

During the primary school years children may grow to exercise Nancy's desire for greater precision in constructive efforts which call for such a discipline. The way in which tools might aid precision was again reflected in ten year old Frank's impatient retort to Anthony who was sawing slats of wood for a puppet theatre they were erecting together. 'For goodness sake get a ruler,' he commanded. 'You'll only waste time and make an awful mess of it if you keep guessing if each side is the same.'

Discovery through dramatizing and pretending

Children from eight to eleven years of age, though exploring more fully their relationships with other people, are still in process of discovering themselves. They are, for instance, intent on discovering the possibilities of improving their physical skills, which seemed ten year old Graham's ambition, when he wrote:

> The thing I like doing best is skating. Ever since I got them I have played with my friends who have got a pair. Nearly every Saturday I play with them. But at the moment, Alan and I are building a cart, so that we can get away from the lads who chase us.
> Most people no how to skate well, the thing I am worst at is starting. I cannot start fast enough yet but I soon will because I keep on trying. I am best at turning sharp. I like turning round best. You have to practice a lot before you get good.

It will be remembered that younger children were seen developing self-awareness. A similar process is at work at this stage as a new consciousness of the self comes into being. One aspect of this personal discovery is recalled by Gwendolen Freeman, who writes:

> But at last, gradually came a time when we began to feel that our consciences were our own. We might keep some things secret. We did not have to expose every fault to the light. I remember a wonderful feeling of freedom when this attitude first occurred to me . . .
> At about this time came the discovery that we could 'cheek' our parents, if we chose the moment well, with impunity. Especially our father. If we could make him laugh it did not matter how 'rude' we were. And the feeling that our parents were some remote deities, always moral and perfect though unintelligible, began blessedly to give way to the idea that they might be human like ourselves.[1]

Out of this growing awareness gradually develops a sense of personal moral responsibility. It is interesting to note from the memories of childhood in several autobiographies that this may arise from a child's realization of his own powers of destruction. Gwendolen Freeman is quoted again, for she clearly remembers

> . . . pausing on the brink of the age when one ceases to kill for fun. One evening I found a large spider in our outside lavatory and killed it meditatively, seeing how the thin dry legs dropped off. It was fascinating because I felt sympathy for the thing at the same time—getting much the same pleasure, I suppose, as sightseers used to get at public executions. Then I began to think that through me that body that had been crawling so determinedly up the distemper

[1] Freeman, Gwendolen, *Children Never Tell*, Allen and Unwin 1949, pp. 50-51.

would never crawl again, and the mystery of death struck me and I
was sorry to have put an end to something for ever and ever. I felt
guilty and yet proud of feeling guilt, since so many people killed
spiders without thinking about it. Afterwards I never killed anything
if I could help it.[1]

Such developments make it possible for these older children to
enter more easily into the feelings of others, though rivalry will at
times be more apparent than sympathy in their relationships with
their peers.

In the junior years imaginative games are one means of growing
in a knowledge of relationships. These may become complex in
their structure and a sustained line of thought, more often absent
in similar activities of younger children, can often be traced in such
play. These characteristics, together with an element of strong
feeling, may be discerned in the play of ten year old Derek who
writes of his play with his friend, Roger:

> The thing I like best is play with my model army of which I have
> 144. Thees solgeirs are bought a inch in hight. I have Germen and
> Britsh. You get them in boxs containing 48 in each of which I buy.
>
> I play with this with my freind Roger he also has some. We play
> on Sautdays we each have toy artilry to march I have to feild guns
> two tanks and sometimes model planes they are all to scale.
>
> Frist we set up artilry than soliders when this is up it looks like
> a reeal battle than Roger starts is morters then the battle starts. The
> battle is deside by which make the other surrder Roger never lets me
> surrder so I fight to the last man.
>
> I like doing this best becours its so like a reraly moden battle.
> But would not like to be in a rerlay one, would you?

Roger's and Derek's drama was in the world of pretence, but
some of the children's dramatizations may be centred in real situations, as happened in the following account of the funeral of a pet
rabbit. This incident is sensitively recalled by Eiluned Lewis, who
tells me that it is based on childhood recollections of herself and
her sister.

> While Dick went to dig a grave behind the nutbushes, they took
> Robert, the wooden horse, with his cart to the rabbit hutch and laid
> poor Jack Baba tenderly in the cart, which he exactly fitted. Then
> they covered him with a black and white handkerchief and laid on
> top of that a white rose which Delia had picked from her own tree.

[1] Op. cit., pp. 53-54.

They pulled Jack Baba all the way from his hutch to the grave. Maurice walked in front, since the horse and cart were his property, and Delia came behind, guiding the cart round the corners. Lucy and Miriam followed: Lucy played tunes on a comb—all the saddest tunes she knew—and Miriam held a bunch of mignonette and some of Jack Baba's favourite radishes.

When they came to the place where the path dips down hill, the procession was difficult to manage, for the cart, being the heavier, went faster than Robert and several times nearly upset. Dick had dug the grave under the hedge and, after Delia had lined it with moss, they buried Jack Baba with the rose, the radishes and the mignonette. But the black-and-white handkerchief was returned to their mother, to keep for another occasion.[1]

The way in which younger children try to work over half understood information in fantasy would seem to be repeated in later childhood in a more elaborate and sustained form. The space age in which they live seems likely to be responsible for the fantasy noted in the account of two ten year old girls' dramatic activities. Sylvia writes:

> The thing I like doing is on a Saturday afternoon, it is kind of club we call it Sisters Adventure. They are four of us. We have are club Just about every Saturday afternoon and some times on a morning if Margaret can come.
> We have lots of fun we kid we are on an island with water around us, last week we pretended that we were going to venes in a rocket but instead of landing on venes we landed on Mars. I like doing it because I like pretending we are other people.

Sylvia incorporates a brief reference to the space travel fantasy into her account of the organization of the club, through which she is able to explore new personal roles and relationships. Her friend, Deborah, describes the experience more fully, including more detail of the fantasy drama.

> The thing I like doing best out of school is going up to Sylvia's house. We have a group of people, and we are always pretending to have an advanture.
> We always do this on Saturday afternoons about three o'clock untill four o'clock. Pam and Kathy are not in this group because they are hardly every here on Saturday afternoons.
> As I told you before we have a little group. Sometimes we pretend that we have landed on Mars or Venus in our anormous space ship.

[1] Lewis, Eiluned, *Dew on the Grass*, Peter Davies 1951, ch. XI, p. 117-118.

Howard, Jennifers brother somtimes pretends to be a ghostly figure
on Mars or Venus. Our anormous space ship is Jennifers hut.
  I like doing this because we get a lot of fun out of it. If I were
at home I would only be morngy because I had nothing to do.

Deborah seems to enjoy experimenting with words, as in the repetition of 'anormous space ship' and the description of Howard, as a
'ghostly figure'.

Sylvia and Deborah belong to the same child-founded club,
which no doubt will call for a degree of co-operation and loyalty on
their part. For it is likely that this club, in common with others run
by children of this age, will have its own secret home-made laws,
whereby the children will encounter the problems of community
living. Peter and Iona Opie[1] have drawn attention to this complex
culture of children evolved over the centuries, which includes traditional games. Writing in the *Sunday Times* they suggested that

> As parents or teachers, most of us are aware of children only when
> they are conforming to or coming up against the adult pattern of
> living: when they are adult-organized, or when they are sharing in
> adult-devised entertainment—the subservient creature crouched in
> front of our TV set. We are liable to gain the impression that when
> children are away from us they are either listless or mischievous.
> Yet the qualities of self-organization, self-discipline and perseverance
> shown by most children of seven to eleven, when they think they
> are on their own, has to be seen to be believed.
> It is possible that we too readily think of a child as a 'good citizen'
> only when he is one of a school football team, or a Scout patrol, or
> undertaking an endurance test. When we suppose that a child is
> unable to entertain himself healthily without adult assistance, we may
> simply be making it more difficult for him to do so.
> Without realizing it, we may be impressing on children the adult
> values of prestige, money-status and desire for visible rewards, even
> in their amusements. For the more children have their 'free time'
> organized for them, and the more they have equipment provided, the
> more they lose the traditional art of self-entertainment.[2]

Perhaps this element of the child culture in the junior years takes
precedence over the channel of pure fantasy in which the younger
child worked over so many of his problems? Its importance would
seem to be too little recognized as a self-preparation for adult life.

[1] Opie, Peter and Iona, *The Language and Lore of School Children*,
Clarendon Press 1959.
[2] *Sunday Times*, 6th August, 1961.

There comes a time in a junior child's development when, if adults are sympathetic, they can use their growing skills in such a way that they experience something of the adult role in reality. Ten year old Stella's mother made this possible for her daughter, when she sometimes permitted her to take over her role and bake a cake for the family. The last sentence in Stella's account of her cake-making suggests that she considers the experience as a contribution to the process of growing up.

I like to bake when I am out of school because it helps my mother a lot if she is very busy. I do it on a Saturday afternoon because if I do it in the morning I would get in Mum's way when she is cleaning the kitchen floor. So I do it in the afternoon.

First I beat two eggs together weight the flour and sugar. Then, I put a certain amount of butter, into a dish and pour the sugar over it. Then place it in a bowl of hot water till it melts. Then I beat it up add the flour and two drops of Lemon Essence to make a Madara cake. I put it in a tin, then put it in the oven to bake for a certain amount of time.

I like doing it because when I grow up I will be able to bake. But some people don't know how to fry bacon and eggs when they are married.

Communicating and recording discovery

A. *The spoken word*

The preceding observations give some indications of the growing importance of speech during this period of childhood. A tendency towards a monologue type of running commentary on their activities, so common among younger children, can still sometimes be heard from older boys and girls when they are, for instance, excited by a new experience. This happened in the response of ten year old boys to magnets and iron filings, the latter being novel to them :

Ian	It is like shaving.
Bobby	I'm pulling it off.
Dennis	Blow, it won't come off. It won't come off.
Paul	It's like combing someone's hair.
Charles	The more I get off, the more it comes on.
Edward	That sounds quite daft.
Charles	It may sound daft, but it is true.
John	I've made a brush (filings hanging at end of magnet). How do you get this stuff off?

Paul	It comes off if you scrape it.
Ian	It sucks it up like a vacuum, doesn't it?
Richard	I say, you can scrape it off with one of these paper clips. Aye, look at that.
Peter	If you put the head of a nail in a pile of filings it picks everything up.
Paul	I must try it. Look, I am transferring some. (He walks over to another desk with the filings hanging on the end of the magnet.)
John	The nail stands up. It is doing a waltz. Aye, it is doing the waltz. It's right good at doing a waltz, I reckon.

The very characteristic use of metaphor or simile in these re-marks is worth noting. It is frequently found in the language of junior children as they, like the younger children, spontaneously tend to fit new experience into the framework of the familiar, a characteristic shared with the poet.

In this seeking to make sense of new experience and knowledge in the medium of the spoken word an element of fantasy may be discerned. This tendency, which has already been noticed in children's speculations in guided discussion and imaginative games, also occurs in spontaneous conversation. An eight year old boy when commenting to me on his sun-tanned skin utilized fantasy in his thought process: 'They say God made the sun but it might have begun by someone lighting a fire here on earth. About 1945 they might have begun it I should have thought. I suppose if they made a sun today they would send it up in a rocket.'

Another characteristic speech in the junior years is the enjoyment of riddles and traditional rhymes. These may include references to topical and religious matters, as the work of Peter and Iona Opie[1] demonstrates. Eight year old Roger provides an illustration in the following conversation:

Roger	Do you know why I'm sorry for God?
Miss M.	No.
Roger	Well, I'll tell you. I'm sorry for him if Jesus is always sitting on his right hand. It must be jolly uncomfortable. I'll ask you another one, shall I? Why do we sing Amen in church?
Miss M.	Tell me why.
Roger	'Cos we sing 'hymns' and not 'hers', see?

[1] Opie, Peter and Iona, *The Language and Lore of School Children*, Clarendon Press 1959.

Reflection suggests that besides the fun of playing with words and 'knowing the answer', which gives such obvious delight to the child, riddles and puns may also represent a transitional stage between the fantasy of earlier years and the growth of logic. They appear to be yet another attempt on the part of children to form thoughts into a meaningful pattern.

During the primary school years, however, children's speech is generally directed towards gaining factual information. They have an apparently insatiable desire to acquire knowledge, and as experiences pose problems their queries indicate an ever increasing desire to discover causes. A few days after experimental play with magnets Penelope commented: 'I've been wondering since you let us have those magnets and iron filings, just what it was that made them stick to the magnets. *Why* does it happen?'

But, in addition to seeking it, children will also offer and share their knowledge. Parents comment on how their growing sons and daughters 'tell me things now'. According to one mother her ten year old daughter frequently prefaced remarks at home with the querying statement: 'Did you know that . . . ?' Another mother reported how when out walking with her eleven year old son on a cloudy day he was reminded of Greek mythology of which he had been reading and told her about the Greek ideas relating to the sky.

It is this increasing delight in seeking and offering knowledge, together with their growing ability to sustain a line of thought, that enables children to enter into discussion where views can be shared and argument can take place. This demands a quickening of mental and linguistic powers, as a child seeks to formulate questions and finds it necessary to clarify his thought in order to communicate some idea or meet the challenge of an opposing opinion.

Mention has been made of increased reliance on reading (p. 44). Some of the children mentioned in this book actually preferred reading to other activities:

> I mostly go to the library in my spare time, sometimes if we are early we stay and read our book. I like going on a Saturday best because we can dawdle on the way and stay longer at the Library.
>
> Why I like going to the library is a simple question mostly because I am very interested in books you can learn things from them.

The need to talk over facts and ideas they have gleaned from books become apparent in the discussion with the older children. It was evident, for instance, in the mistaken idea George voiced in his query: 'You know the shape of stars. Well, how do they get the lines making them into animals and things?' (p. 47). Other children cleared up the mystery for him, by indicating that the signs of the Zodiac were not representations of objective fact. The confusion caused in eleven year old Jonathan's mind through his access to books on mythology was voiced in his query: 'How did the ancient gods like Thor disappear when the people believed in the one true God?'

Books, however, not only supply information, they also tell stories and so may answer questions of a different nature. Marjorie Hourd has called attention to the way in which literature may help children in sorting out the bewilderment which happenings in life around them may present.

> It is a life which is utterly baffling to them and which needs as much interpretation as the world of things and natural phenomena. Literature is as much a means of this interpretation and a criticism of life to a child as it is to us.[1]

B. *The written word*

An example of how spontaneous writing may occur is in Eiluned Lewis's description of a service written for the funeral of a rook, squirrel and field mouse, the influence of a Latin lesson, which immediately preceded the writing of the service, being apparent. Eiluned Lewis relates how after it had been decided that the service ought not to be about God or Jesus,

> Lucy fetched an old exercise book and a pencil, and they ran to their favourite place, under a sprawling apple tree beside the river. There, between them, they wrote a liturgy, to be used on all occasions by dogs, rabbits, mice and other animals, including toys and particularly, said David, toy soldiers. It began quite cheerfully:

O to the dog of dogs,
O to the rabbit of rabbits
Let us pray and to the septar of the king of the sea.
Rex.
Omnes veri Regem et Reginam amant.
Praise ye them and glorify them.
O ye children of men, honour them and serve them.
In the name of the queen of the fairies and the king of rabbits.

ARMEN

[1] Op. cit., p. 40.

O dog of dogs, have mercy upon us sinners,
Be good to us, O King, and make us joyful;
Save us all from breaking and illness, O King of the princes of
dogs, and bless the holy one here present, and save our King,
O King of dogs.

Praise O praise our doggy king,
Praise him through this long dark night
With the joy of sweet daylight,
Through the holy dog of dogs.

ARMEN

Now comes more war that we may use the valour we have got, and
we pray that we might like the men of days gone by, many of
them dead. In the name of the queen of the fairies and the king
of the rabbits.

ARMEN

Many of the battles we cannot remember, as most of the most
brave are dead now, but there are a few remaining; but if we only
acted as they do, if we die is it not something to be read about in
this book, and recorded for every one in the mind of the holy dog.[1]

This bit of writing illustrates once more how children weave their
experiences into a pattern. Here familiarity with the language and
practices of the church is woven into a knowledge of Latin and an
acquaintance with fairy stories.

Both imaginative and factual writing will take their place with
junior children, who will differ in ability and the type of writing
they most enjoy but may grow to appreciate the need for accuracy
and clarity if their writing is to communicate ideas and information
to others. That older children also express their thought in poetry is
evident in the work of Marjorie Hourd and Gertrude Cooper.[2]

During these years the function of a dictionary may be recognized, for children often become interested in words. They want to
discover origins of words and pose other queries

Where did the word ten come from?
Why do we join the a and e in Julius Caesar?
Will you please explain the pronunciation of the word 'picture'.

---

[1] Op. cit., ch. XI, pp. 119-120.
[2] Hourd, M. L. and Cooper, G. E., *Coming into Their Own*, Heinemann
1959.

But there is no doubt that

> The quality of children's writing will be partly determined by the
> help they are given in savouring experience to the full. Accurate
> observation is as important as subsequent discussion about what has
> been seen.[1]

c. *Picture-making*

Junior children enjoy picture-making and though they will become increasingly concerned that their illustrations 'look right',
their pictures can also convey intense feelings. Reference may be
made here to an occasion when a teacher suggested to a group of
eight year olds that they might write something which would tell
other people about God, and if they felt it would help they could
draw a picture. The pictures drawn showed a development of
thought from the superhuman to the supernatural idea of God
indicated in a selection of accompanying comments given below.[2]

1. One boy drew a picture of God which reflected the space-age
in which the child lived, for the deity was clothed in a kind of
space-suit. His written comments were typical of many of the
descriptions:

> God has long hair and a beard and he is like an ordinary man.

2. Another child regarded God in human terms but seated on a
throne in the sky above the earth, surrounded by angels. The child
wrote:

> God is a holy person. He sits on a throne with a toasting fork. He
> has blue eyes, long hair and a long beard.

3. Two children drew pictures which were of a semi-human
nature.

A boy introduced the idea of half-spirit, drawing a handless and
legless figure, but using very strong colours. He wrote:

> God looks like half man, half spirit. Hes got black hair and a
> black beard.

In contrast, one girl's picture was in soft colours, the figure of God,
though handless and legless, was surrounded by white, giving a
mystical feeling. She wrote:

> God is white and he has a white beard with long white hair.

[1] *Primary Education*, HMSO 1959, p. 161.
[2] See front and back cover.

4. Some of the children thought of God as a cloud but having some human characteristics, among these were a boy who drew an outline of a cloud above a city street and wrote:

I think God is like a cloud with an eye and mouth.

And a girl who drew a black cloud and wrote:

God is like a cloud but he can speak.

5. One child drew a red and orange cloud set in a jet black sky above emerald green grass. She wrote:

I think God is like a coloured cloud.

A further development of thought was seen in the comment of a ten year old boy when it was suggested that he might write something which would tell people about God and could, if he wished, draw some kind of picture. He said, 'I couldn't draw a picture because you can't see God. You can feel him, though, giving his blessing on you.' When asked how, he replied: 'It is a sort of goodness you feel going into you.'

Older children may thus reveal in pictorial form the fact that they, like the younger children, are working over impressions. This was also evident in two pictures done as a co-operative effort by two eleven year old boys, entitled, 'If war should come' and 'Invasion from outer space'. When asked what had made them think of drawing these pictures, one replied: 'We thought we would do a picture about the future instead of history.' Asked where they had obtained ideas about the future they said: 'Well, there is all this trouble about Berlin and things like that, and Russia is letting off all these bombs.' One of the boys wrote these explanatory notes which indicate the content of the pictures:

If war should come

The whole picture   The picture is of a research station and united nations building and a missile station in America.

Section One   The first section of the picture is of the homes of the people who work at the research station. The fall-out shelter in the corner is for the general public to use (if you do not know, a fall-out shelter is a shelter to protect people from radio-activity).

Section Two   The second section is of the barracks for the
army staff only, that includes the soldiers. The
people you can see dressed in civilian clothes are
people who have been taken from the public
fall-out shelter because there was know room for
them. The jet pilot talking to the M.P. is
surrposed to have brought a message telling them
of a similar attack on Britain.

Section Three   There is nothing much of interest in section
three. The small hut is where two soldiers or
more are posted to guard the entrance to the
research station. The fall-out shelter is a private
shelter for the united nations when they are at
a meeting.

Section Four   The most interesting picture of all. It shows the
united nations building and a missile station. The
chauffer of one of the deligates or members of
the united nations pulling an alarm to warn the
united nations in a meeting that an attack has
been launched againsed them. The fall-out
shelter in the corner is an extra one.

Invasion from Outer space

Picture One   In this picture there is a grocer's shop which is
being attacked by monsters. On the roof there
are two striped monsters fighting because they
disagreed about whom they were going to kill
in the shops and houses.

Picture Two   In this picture there are several space ships in
the air and one is controlling some of the
monsters from the ground. There are several
men from the army trying to destroy the monsters and one of the men is about to be eaten.

Picture Three   In this picture there is a jet coming into land
with a few of the invasion leaders. Nearby there
is a very large space ship which contains a control room and laboratory for making dehydrated
monsters and a gas for killing people.

Picture Four   In this picture the most important thing is an
army tank which is being brought up to try and
destroy a control ship. There is also a man
being shrunk by a ray from the space-ship.

One of these eleven year old boys in his leisure-time at home later portrayed in symbolic form his idea of good and evil, which is an unusual reminder of the pleasure juniors may derive from pattern-making. The design appeared to be an abstract form of the conceptions in the picture 'Invasion from outer space' and probably reflected the influence of both television and the blueprints on which the boy had seen his engineer father working.

As in other modes of communication children in their art will develop their powers only if the atmosphere encourages sincerity of feeling and, at the same time, sensitive guidance is given, for

> Like all forms of language, its use involves effort: there must be respect for the materials employed if they are to be properly handled as instruments of ideas. Above all, children have to be helped to observe and see; and their school environment and their experiences with it should together lead them to see with a growing acuteness and discernment, with finer appreciation and subtler feeling . . .[1]

To summarize

Junior children continue the search for meaning through question and further physical exploration of the world around them. Dissatisfaction with crude results, and a desire for greater accuracy, give rise to more thorough speculative thought and action. Mental development, together with extended experience, brings about a clearer conception of self and other people and makes easier the interchange of ideas and a growing willingness to entertain other points of view. Fantasy and drama play a part in the sorting out of their ideas, but the growth of a seemingly insatiable interest in factual information becomes increasingly apparent. A developing competence in oral and written expression is noted and reading ability makes possible a greater degree of independence in obtaining answers to queries which can be culled from books. The manner in which junior children seek to deepen their understanding illustrates clearly the observation of Professor Jeffreys, who noted that '. . . as children's ingenuity constantly demonstrates, the human mind seeks *meaning* at all costs'.[2]

[1] *Primary Education*, HMSO 1959, p. 221.
[2] Jeffreys, M. C. V., *Mystery of Man*, Pitman 1957, p. 76.

3 *The Deepening of Understanding during the Primary School Years*

LET US REMIND ourselves at this point of Professor Jeffreys' suggestion that 'Religious truth is normal experience understood at fullest depth'.[1] In the light of this principle I propose to make a brief summary of some of the ways in which the interaction of experience and thought may deepen children's understanding during the primary school years.

Exploring and constructing

The most marked feature of the younger children's exploration of the world around them was the way in which they seem continually urged by some inner compulsion to make personal discoveries. Observation of a similar compulsion led Frank Kendon to suggest that the

> History of early childhood is really a list of first occasions, a list of minute discoveries whose significance was felt but not understood then, a list of new experiences. For the germ of spiritual life with which we began can only grow as it gets nourishment from the world in which it was sparked, and of its food it makes its own bulk. Its food is experience.[2]

Such discoveries were seen in the silent experimental handling of materials and objects, as Paul played with the sand (p. 19) or Robert handled the stones which he removed from the nursery school nature table (p. 24). This experimental activity may cause

[1] Op. cit., p. 118.
[2] Kendon, Frank, *The Small Years*, OUP 1950, p. 160.

children to examine the constructive possibilities of materials and objects. Michael's and Rachel's use of scrap materials for the purpose of making a bridge and windmill (p. 26 and p. 27) and Colin's experimental manipulations of the pulley were examples (p. 23). They illustrate how young children will exercise persistence whilst endeavouring on their own initiative to deepen their comprehension of the world of things. An activity of this kind may also involve a child in a valuation of his actions in the light of experience. Michael realized that his bridge was not large enough for his boat to pass under, but was content, at the time, to recognize but not overcome the particular problem, though his remarks indicated that he knew the reasons for it (p. 26). Colin, however, whose problem was solved more simply, tried twisting the string more tightly round the door handle when his first effort to keep the bucket in position failed (p. 23). Rachel voluntarily undertook the laborious processes necessary to master the difficulties involved in making sails for her windmill which would turn round (p. 27).

Older children can also be observed in similar spontaneous reactions to materials and things in their search for meaning. But their physical and mental development, together with their wider experience, may mean that they are in a position to undertake more complex ventures. Their eagerness to accept the challenge of pitting themselves against natural forces was noted in James's efforts in learning to swim (p. 62) and Stuart's pride in his dam-building (p. 64). Such experiences would seem to be the kind of boyhood joys Wordsworth had in mind when he wrote

> Thus oft amid those fits of vulgar joy
> Which, through all seasons, on a child's pursuits
> Are prompt attendants, 'mid that giddy bliss
> Which like a tempest, works along the blood
> And is forgotten; even then I felt
> Gleams like the flashing of a shield;—the earth
> And common face of Nature spake to me
> Rememberable things . . .[1]

James Kenward shows how junior children will become deeply absorbed and exert much persistence in overcoming problems encountered in their self-directed experiments. That one discovery may initiate a further experiment is illustrated in his description of the manner in which the 'Elastic Grand' was evolved from the initial

[1] Wordsworth, William, *The Prelude*, J. H. Dent 1940, Book 1, pp. 581-588.

discovery that stretched elastic, when touched with the fingers, produced a sound.[1] In such concrete situations children are seen to examine their efforts critically, seeking for cause and effect, which may lead to a refinement of techniques in order to obtain better results. In noticing this characteristic of childhood, Ruth Griffiths observes that:

> Development consists in a process of continually measuring one's strength against external forces. There is a need to strive, to overcome, to submit. The child experiments continually and learns often by hard and bitter experience those directions in which he can succeed and those circumstances to which he must yield.[2]

She then poses the question that this process of experimentation continues throughout life by asking:

> Are men not continually measuring their strength against the universe, striving to wrest from it its secrets, or we may say, striving to create it anew. And are there not times when they have to accept the limitations of their powers, and submit to the realization of the real, the final, the inevitable? Such are landmarks in the development of the mind.[3]

It is during experimentations in these primary school years that children come to see the need to acquire increasing skill in the use of tools. The mastery of such a skill as measurement, for example, may enable a child to enter into new realms of discovery, for it has been truly stated that

> . . . Every time we assimilate a tool to our body our identity undergoes some change; our person expands into new modes of being.[4]

The importance of such a process needs no emphasis, for

> . . . all . . . mental life by which we surpass the animals is evoked in us as we assimilate the articulate framework of our culture.[5]

Here may be reported an observation of two brothers aged five and nine years of age, since it clearly illustrates the development of thought occurring in these years. The manner in which the nine year old boy assisted his younger five year old brother, who was

---

[1] Op. cit., pp. 82-83.   [2] Op. cit., p. 120.   [3] Op. cit., p. 120.
[4] Polanyi, Michael, *The Study of Man*, Routledge and Kegan Paul 1959, p. 31.
[5] Ibid., p. 31.

constructing an edifice with bricks, indicates how reliance on visual comparison, or comparison with parts of the body as noted previously,[1] may gradually be replaced by the felt need for a standard unit, such as a footrule. The reactions of the younger child also makes clear that mental development as well as experience is involved in the growth of understanding. It is important to realize that the stages of development represented by these two boys constitute a continuous and overlapping process, each stage being built upon previous experiences. Such examples emphasize Nathan Isaacs' statement that

All the way through, further integration can only be built on effective integration.[2]

A five year old boy built a tower of twelve bricks, then turned to the observer and said: 'You know you just must put each brick quite straight, or else they all fall over.' He went on: 'I'm going to build another tower just as high as this one. You watch me.'

It was interesting to note the way he decided that the towers were of identical height. He stood back viewing his achievement and then, seemingly as a check, he touched the top of one tower with his hand, moving his hand slowly over the space between the two towers to the top bricks of the other one. He then stood by one of the towers and putting his finger on the part of his body which coincided with the top bricks he went over to the other one to compare it. 'There,' he announced with satisfaction, 'they're both the same.'

His nine year old brother joined him and said: 'I'll show you how to measure them properly.' The nine year old took a footrule and placed it alongside each tower twice, commenting: 'There, two feet you see, so you are quite right, they are the same.'

After a moment's reflection the nine year old resumed his measuring operations with the footrule and went on to say: 'As a matter of fact each of these bricks is two inches high, so you really need only measure one brick, then count them.' He proceeded to do this, the five year old joining in. 'Twelve, you see, so twelve twos are twenty-four, and that's two feet because there are twelve inches in one foot.'

The five year old watched, listening patiently, but immediately afterwards he repeated his own mode of measurement by passing his hands over from the top of one tower to another.

[1] Observation of Michael, p. 26.
[2] Isaacs, Nathan, *The Growth of Understanding in Young Children*, ESA 1961, p. 35.

Dramatizing and pretending

As well as coming to terms with the world of things, children are faced with the need to come to an understanding of people, including themselves. The younger children's absorption in such discoveries was made amply clear in their spontaneous activities. One way in which this was demonstrated was the manner in which individual children used the same medium in different ways, according to their personal needs. David's use of the water for playing out the role of the 'fish and chip lady' (p. 20) and Angus' manipulation of the co-operative brick-play to enact the role of 'wounded soldier' (p. 33) were two such instances.

Fantasy can frequently be discerned in young children's attempts to achieve some coherence in experience. Sometimes it is very difficult, indeed impossible, for an observer to trace any sustained line of thought in the comments which accompany such play. Occasions like the sand-play of the group of five year olds (p. 32), in which powerful emotions were integrated, give a glimpse of children's inner life. Marjorie Hourd in discussing the function of play states that

> Play serves a physical and a social end; it develops the child's body muscles and he needs other children for its happy fulfilment; but it goes deeper than this. He is also expressing an individual psychology; his own conflicts; his own perceptions, his own incipient reasoning. When he is building with bricks, we do not know merely by watching him what deep desire is being satisfied by the towering summits of his castle.[1]

Reference to autobiography or our own recollections of childhood may help us to realize the nature of some of the unexpressed perplexity which may trouble children. A student provided an example in writing of a childhood dream which occurred frequently after her grandmother's death, when she feared that her mother, too, would go away and never return:

> I used to have a very bad dream shortly after my grandmother died. I can remember in my dream my mother walking down a path with a garden on either side. Then opening a gate she passed through it. Never once did she look back, although I called to her. When I got to the gate I could not open it. I sat down and cried. I woke up crying.

[1] Hourd, Marjorie, *The Education of the Poetic Spirit*, p. 25.

This dream is as vivid in my mind today as if it happened only yesterday. I shall never forget the fear and sorrow I experienced and the overwhelming relief when I woke up and realized that it was only a dream. I never told anyone what the dream was about.

From time to time children may reveal their thoughts as Donald did when he enquired a few days after playing with magnets: 'Do angels pull the clouds along with magnets?' Marion's remarks about her baby sister whilst drawing her pictures also gave an indication of the kind of problem she was trying to solve (p. 39).

In the junior years children continue to explore problems concerned with themselves and other people through dramatization, which may sometimes take the form of fantasy. This was plain in Derek's account of the soldier-play (p. 68) and the drama of the Sisters' Adventure Club described by Sylvia and Deborah (p. 69). Increasing attempts at co-operation are made during these years, often worked out in the sphere of traditional child-culture, including games which children themselves organize. The realization of the fallibility of the adult and a growing awareness of their own powers bring about both a more critical attitude and the possibility of a deeper understanding through the exercise of imagination. It was such developments that Marjorie Hourd had in mind when, in commenting on the junior school years, she pointed out that the stage of pure identification having passed

> . . . the child will not be compelled to be Cinderella or Jack-the-Giant-Killer only because he is representing his own humility or his own assertion; instead, he also looks upon the characters he meets in books with imaginative sympathy.[1]

It would appear that as the awareness of others deepens, moral conceptions are formulated more clearly. This was shown in some of the searching questions and the trend of the discussions of the older children.[2] The reading of autobiography also provided examples in which the sense of responsibility for conduct appeared to grow alongside a child's awareness of his own power.[3] Further evidence is given by Frank Kendon, who describes incidents in his own childhood which depict three stages in this gradual dawning of a sense of personal responsibility. The first is typical of the stage when a belief in magic predominates in the children's thought:

[1] Op. cit., pp. 27, 28.
[2] Cf. pp. 45-58.
[3] See reference to Gwendolen Freeman's experience quoted on p. 67.

We used to believe, with other country children, that to kill a beetle would bring rain; and in our innocent days we blamed one another for killing beetles—not because of waste or cruelty, but because we liked fine weather.[1]

The second shows how, having exerted his destructive power, he was concerned not with the victim of his impulsive action but with the punishment which might follow. He had chased a cock and thrown a piece of wood, which caused the bird to be stunned, though the boy, at the time, believed the bird to be dead.

I left him there, but I feared only for myself, lest my father would find out that by my act he was one chick short . . . it can be imagined what release from guilt I felt, when, the day afterwards, I saw the same fellow clucking to the hens . . . none the worse for my blow.

This was not murder, and I was, at that point, in my life, too young to have much imaginative sympathy. The apparent death of the cock had merely threatened to expose me.[2]

The third refers to three or four years later when the death of a wren was caused by a playmate, who deliberately threw a stone at the bird. Frank Kendon relates how through this incident he became aware of 'a new and troublesome faculty'.

Through all these long days of our first decade beauty had shone about us and love had poured itself into us, largely unknown to us because we had never known the absence of these things. The spirit had silently been preparing that we might bear sorrows, and that very moment, when we looked at the dead wren (though there were others, no doubt less memorable), becomes the moment of initiation. I began to hate the waste of flowers picked and thrown away, and to feel myself guilty for slashing nettles, or parsley heads or bluebells with a stick.[3]

Communicating and recording

The importance of spoken language through which young children may endeavour to clarify their experiences was very evident in the preceding pages. This may occur through the comment, question, and discussion which so often accompany their self-chosen activities, endorsing the truth of an official suggestion that

[1] Op. cit., p. 154.   [2] Op. cit., p. 153.   [3] Ibid., p. 154.

The younger the child the greater the need for words . . . to be rooted in first-hand sensory experience, if he is to understand the language that describes the sensible world and appreciate later the many metaphorical extensions of meaning.[1]

Discovering meaning in the spoken word is a vital step towards seeing the significance of the written word. Picture-making which forms a bridge between speaking and writing in the early days has been seen to continue to take its place in the communication of facts, thoughts and feelings in later childhood. Although the junior children have a greater command of the spoken word their need to have opportunity to question and discuss was also made clear in these observations, for the dangers of mere 'book-knowledge' became very apparent in talking to the more intelligent juniors. It nevertheless remains true to say that

. . . a junior school child is often active even without moving about. A great deal of his mental activity goes on through language—in thinking, speaking, writing, and reading. He can use language to plan ahead and to re-live a past experience, often described in a long narrative. He is able to write and record what he would say, and through reading lives imaginatively in the exploits of other people at other times and places. His questions are more pertinent than before, and his knowledge becomes more definite. His world, therefore, enlarges at a great rate and, with encouragement and opportunity, he enters upon his exploration of it, physically, intellectually and imaginatively, with confidence and zest.[2]

[1] *Primary Education*, HMSO 1959, p. 141.
[2] Ibid., pp. 56-57.

PART TWO

Some Reflections on Children in Search of Meaning

1 *The Infant School Years*

Up to this point I have presented observations of children engaged in their search for meaning, indicating their modes of dealing with problems. Let us consider whether the material collected offers any guidance for those engaged in religious and scientific education in the primary school years.

The significance of personal discovery and sensory experience

The observations show how the beginning of understanding of the world around them comes to children through their urge to make personal discoveries of their environment. The nature and depth of these early experiences are crystallized in Kathleen Raine's poem about childhood:

> Then I had no doubt
> That snowdrops, violets, all creatures, I myself
> Were lovely, were loved, were love.
> Look, they said.
> And I had only to look deep into the heart,
> Dark, deep into the violet, and there read,
> Before I knew of any word for flower or love,
> The flower, the love, the word.
> They never wearied of telling their being; and I
> Asked of the rose only more rose, the violet
> More violet; untouched by time
> No flower withered or flame died,
> But posed in its own eternity, until the looker moved
> On to another flower, opening its entity.[1]

[1] Raine, Kathleen, *Collected Poems of Kathleen Raine*, 'Exile', Hamish Hamilton 1956.

Whilst engaged in their explorations of the immediate world children are confronted with mysteries which may cause them to probe further by means of action or the spoken question. Such a situation roused five year old Mark, when the bricks with which he played continually fell, to make the exasperated enquiry: '*Why* does this silly bridge keep falling down?' and his playmate to make the speculative suggestion that a different mode of building might solve the problem (p. 25). Thus revision of judgment and a change of technique grew out of observation, refined through personal insight in the course of experience. This attitude towards phenomena is the basis of scientific curiosity, since the scientist cannot be content with general vague impressions, for 'he requires exact details which will enable him to discover relations of forms or functions'.[1] But like the five year old boy, the scientist at times makes a speculative leap, which in turn reveals new problems and insights. Isaac Newton saw reflected in his scientific work the discoveries of boyhood:

> I do not know how I may appear to the world; but to myself I seem to have been only like a boy, playing on the seashore, and diverting myself, in now and then, finding another pebble or prettier shell than ordinary, while the great ocean of truth lay all undiscovered before me.[2]

But it is not always realized that these early personal discoveries, so fundamental to a knowledge of the world in which we live, are also significant for religious thought and enquiry, for as Andrew Osborn, when commenting on the views of Schleiermacher, pointed out:

> Sense perception lies at the basis of religious experiences, for if we had no knowledge of the outside world we could not know God. Then again knowledge rises from the unconscious to the conscious and the possibility of exercising reasoning depends upon the growth of consciousness.[3]

Ronald Goldman stressed this fact in his study of the development of religious thinking in childhood and adolescence:

> Clearly religion and life in the early years are so interwoven they are indistinguishable. The child has his first sensory experience of the

[1] Osborn, Andrew R., *Schleiermacher and Religious Education*, OUP 1934, pp. 50-51.
[2] Brewster, David, *Memoirs of Sir Isaac Newton*, 1855, Vol. 11, p. 407.
[3] Ibid., p. 49.

material world in which people are at first undifferentiated. He then forms general percepts and concepts based upon these experiences, symbolizing them, first in images and later, when he learns to use language, in verbal images or words. The whole structure of religious thinking is therefore based upon what Havighurst calls 'vicarious' experience. There are no definite religious sensations and perceptions, separate from the child's other sensations and perceptions. Religious thinking is the process of generalizing from various experiences, previous perceptions and already held concepts to an interpretative concept of the activity and nature of the divine. Because of this it is not possible to supply specific first steps in the religious experiences of the young child, other than by enriching his general experience.[1]

The interpretation of experience

Young children will attempt to integrate whatever comes into their experience into a meaningful pattern, be it angels and magnets, sun and rockets, seeds and babies, aeroplanes and heaven, God and shops, Jesus and baby-sitters. This analogy-making propensity noted again and again in this investigation is at the very root of creative thought. We should surely consciously enlist it in the service of religious and scientific education. For instance, although young children cannot appreciate analogies concerning Palestinian life and thought, the expression of their own analogies with regard to their own environment may pave the way for later insight into the metaphorical element in biblical literature. Opportunities may occur when children recollect their own experiences, as it did with a group of six year olds who had been collecting autumn leaves. On returning to the class-room the children shared their memories of the experience. Brian said that he remembered the sound the leaves made when he trod upon them. Whereupon Peter remarked: 'Oh, yes, it reminded me of the sound of the little waves at the sea,' which prompted Elizabeth to comment: 'But, when it's raining and you walk through the leaves, then they are just like cereal with lots of milk on it.'

Sometimes children's interpretations indicate a need for a wider experience as in the case of the five year old in East London, who thought that the churns of milk on a lorry were going to 'fill up the cows', as he had seen the automatic milk machines in the city streets replenished by men. Sometimes they indicate confusion caused by ideas introduced by adults, seen in Ian's attempt to deal with the

[1] Goldman, Ronald, *Religious Thinking from Childhood to Adolescence*, p. 15.

idea of the Holy Ghost (p. 33), or other children's puzzlement about the divinity of Jesus and ideas of heaven. Such interpretations remind us that premature instruction may be adding to a child's problems, for, as Ronald Goldman's research has exposed, children may not always learn what we intend to teach.[1] This is not to suggest that children should only experience what is solely within their ken, for such a policy would be impracticable, and indeed undesirable, in the ordinary course of life. But as adults we have a responsibility to exercise sensitivity in the choice of planned experiences. Watered down versions of Bible stories, for example, can easily create misunderstandings and impede later comprehension. This fact is often mentioned in adults' recollections of their early instruction.[2]

Although guidance given by modern research must be heeded seriously, it may happen that a teacher feels able to introduce material apparently more suited to a later stage if associated with children's experiences. We must, however, constantly keep in mind the danger of reinforcing children's immature notions and hindering later interests through over-familiarity. That these principles apply to the formation of scientific as well as religious conceptions, was forcibly illustrated to me when I was carrying out experimental tests regarding children's ideas of measurement based on Jean Piaget's work.[3]

Scientific and religious conceptions can be seen to grow alongside one another from the totality of a child's experience, both subject to the same principles of true learning, which, Nathan Isaacs states,

> . . . depends upon children being able to integrate further elements into schemes in their minds which are integrated already and into which the new elements naturally and continuously *fit*. No formal material will do that, nor any situations taken out of their context for instruction's sake. Nothing will serve but what can be made meaningful to the child: that is, by being joined up with what is meaningful to him already; real felt problems, and also real felt *discoveries* about the way to solve them.[4]

Young children's need to grow in understanding of the immediate world must be recognized as the basis of religious and scientific thought and enquiry.

[1] Goldman, Ronald, *Religious Thinking from Childhood to Adolescence*, ch. 15.   [2] See Appendix A.
[3] Piaget, Jean, *The Child's Conception of Geometry*, Routledge and Kegan Paul 1960.
[4] Isaacs, Nathan, *The Growth of Understanding in the Young Child*, p. 39.

A sense of the mysterious

Schleiermacher recognized in young children's ceaseless search for meaning the seed of religious thought and enquiry. In one of his *Discourses* he notes that

> Children search everywhere for something surpassing the accustomed phenomena and the light play of life. However many earthly objects are presented for their knowing, there still seems to be another sense unnourished. This is the first stirrings of religion. A secret, inexplicable presentiment urges them past the riches of this world.[1]

Whether we believe that these inner stirrings prompt, or are prompted by, the twin elements of curiosity and wonder, young children's seemingly unquenchable persistence in their pursuit of meaning is very apparent. Wordsworth, too, recognized this quality of children's response to the world around them:

> The thought of our past years in me doth breed
> Perpetual benediction: not indeed
> For that which is most worthy to be blest;
> Delight and liberty, the simple creed
> Of childhood, whether busy or at rest,
> With new-fledged hope still fluttering in his breast: —
> Not for these I raise
> The song of thanks and praise;
> But for those obstinate questionings
> Of sense and outward things,
> Fallings from us, vanishings;
> Blank misgivings of a creature
> Moving about in worlds not realized,
> High instincts before which our mortal nature
> Did tremble like a guilty thing surprised.[2]

From this elemental sense of the mysterious, moments of wonder akin to worship seem occasionally to arise. These occasions may be individual and momentary. They may well possess more of the true essence of worship than the usual adult-directed forms, in so far as the younger children are concerned: perhaps we should become

[1] Schleiermacher, *Discourses on Religion*, trans. by J. Oman, London 1893, p. 125.
[2] Wordsworth, William, 'Ode on Intimations of Immortality', *Selected Poems of William Wordsworth*, ed. Roger Sharrock, Heinemann 1963, pp. 107 ff.

more sensitive to this characteristic of child nature in our religious education? Such wonder was inherent in Alison's story of the little girl who praised the sun (p. 36); in six year old Margaret's response to a bowl of opening daffodil buds when she exclaimed to herself: 'How very good of God.' It was present in John's surprised tone, when coming in from a village playground he told his teacher 'I've just heard lots of silence out there'; or the silent observation of falling snow by Maurice and Jeremy through the nursery window (p. 37). It was evident in Sally's puzzled amazement when she caused iron filings to move by using a magnet, and exclaimed: 'Look, they're wriggling, they're wriggling' (p. 22). Seven year old Paul attempted to communicate his sense of wonder in his painting of the healing of the blind man, as Linda of the same age did when she wrote

> One morning in
> lark song I heard a lovely
> tone, The dark was
> gowing the sun was coming.

Or on another occasion

> One night very early, still light
> Two loveing Doves came flying
> To give spirit to everyone
> As they flew we saw them
> From our window

Such sensitive awareness, in which thought and feeling merge, at times touching the fringe of the mystical, may well remain unexpressed because frequently uncommunicable in the medium of words. But memories of poets and others suggest that children enter into such experiences, which are frequently associated with the natural world and birth and death. Frank Kendon recalls his sensations in a wood.

Leaves touched me; small as I was they swept my freckled face and red hair. I looked with a kind of breathless but friendly awe at the commonest sights—the yellow pimpernel, the bluebell seedheads, the soft springy dry turkey mosses. I heard the leaves move, I heard the dry twigs snap, I heard my breath and my heart. I was always afraid in a wood, but not with an evil fear, unless sometimes I let it get the upper hand of me.[1]

[1] Kendon, Frank, *The Small Years*, p. 15.

Walter de la Mare tells us how he became conscious of the transient nature of a flower when his joy in the discovery of a convolvulus was changed into sadness at its swift wilting.

> . . . its cool dark heart shaped leaves and waxen vase-like simplicity awoke in me a curious wonder and delight, and I remember the shimmering seeding grasses bowing in the windy sunshine when I lay rapturously watching them one morning in a later June. I plucked the flower out of the hedge to take it home to my mother. But when I came into the house it had wreathed itself into a spiral as if into a shroud. And when I realized it would never more be enticed out of it again, I burst into tears.[1]

Early emotional attitudes

These quotations are a reminder of the intensity of a young child's emotional responses to life. If we wish to help younger children in their search for meaning we must provide channels through which emotional expression and development can take place. Here the significance of play, including creative activities, is clear. We must also respect children's need to retreat into fantasy as one means of sifting out the impressions which crowd in on them. Its function is described by Ruth Griffiths:

> Like those simple animalculae that stretch out long pseudopodia into the surrounding water in search of food, retiring afterwards into a state of apparent passivity while digestion takes place, so does the child seek experience, and having come into contact with reality in some form, retires within himself to understand and consolidate what he has acquired. He cannot tackle a problem at once, immediately, even such problems as seem insignificant to us. This is surely the meaning of childhood; time is needed for adaptation.[2]

But though we may value the creative part fantasy may take in child thought it is interesting to learn that

> . . . certain comparative studies have shown that in an environment of free interchange and discussion magical representations decline rapidly in favour of rational representation, whereas they persist much longer in an authoritative environment.[3]

[1] de la Mare, Walter, *Early One Morning*, Faber and Faber 1935, p. 35.
[2] Griffiths, Ruth, *A Study of Imagination in Early Childhood*, p. 174.
[3] Tanner, J. M. and Inhelder, Barbel, *Discussions on Child Development*, Tavistock Publications, Vol. 1, 1953, p. 85.

D

Instances of this are seen in this book in the way in which opportunity for first-hand experience and the interchange of thought may
help children to sort out their ideas. Examples are the manner in
which John contributed to Bobby's knowledge (p. 16), Sally
learned about magnetic forces (p. 22) and older children expressed
doubts in discussion.

Since the intensity of their emotional life makes young children
very susceptible to impressions we have a responsibility with regard
to the quality of the emotions aroused by *all* experiences we deliberately offer them, for

> . . . who shall parcel out
> His intellect by geometric rules,
> Split like a province into round and square?
> Who knows the individual hour in which
> His habits were first sown, even as a seed,
> Who that shall point, as with a wand, and say,
> 'This portion of the river of my mind
> Came from yon fountain?'[1]

Adult recollections of childhood suggest that the religious conceptions presented to children are often tinged with sentimentality
which may thwart that deepening of understanding which leads to
an experience of religious truth, and may also cause an ever-
widening gap between science and religion. This is a tendency we
need to guard against in worship as well as in the religious instruction of young children.

In what ways do children give us clues to the way in which
positive attitudes to worship may be established? Incidental occasions, when children are confronted with the mysterious, have been
seen as one entry into the meaning of worship. The fact that they
often occur in connection with responses to the natural world may
present openings for corporate worship. The children themselves
may give the lead. I well remember an occasion when a sweep
visited a class of six year olds to talk to them about his work. He
accepted the invitation of one of the children to see an almond tree
in full bloom in the school grounds. Whilst out-of-doors a child
suggested: 'Let's have a thank you time out here.' The same child
turned to the sweep, who had closed his eyes and bowed his head
in readiness for prayer, and said: 'If I were you I would keep your
eyes open and look up today.' Other modes in which prayer may

[1] Wordsworth, William, *The Prelude*, J. M. Dent 1940, Book II, 203-210.

take place have been suggested by young children, who had grown to realize that prayer could take different forms: 'Can we have a quiet time and say prayers inside us today?' 'Let's whisper prayers today: I want to talk to God on my own.' The teacher may be asked to contribute: 'You say the thank yous today.' 'You say the prayer you told us the other day.' It is worth noting that student recollections of prayer in early childhood indicate that their own spontaneous private expressions were more meaningful than the prayers taught them by adults:

> I used to enjoy praying by myself as a child and would spend hours in the garden shed composing prayers and saying them to God in a very conversational manner.
>
> The prayers I made up myself had more meaning for me because I understood them.

It was Mother Julian of Norwich, who said 'our good Lord showed me that it is his full pleasure that a silly soul come to him naked, plain and homely.'

There may be occasions when prayer in its usual forms may be inappropriate. But do we appreciate when we permit children to converse with us that 'Such an exchange is nearer to the root of prayer than recitation into the void'?[1] The very quality of our listening may offer a channel through which children may grow to know the meaning of true communion and come to possess, as a fifteen year old girl suggested, 'something to fill out the words with'.[2]

A six year old girl, in voicing her opinion, confirmed my own feeling that the beginning of the morning was not necessarily the best time for young children's worship. 'Couldn't we have thank you time at the end of the morning because then we'd have lots more things to talk to God about?' she enquired. We may also consider whether children might not gain more if worship more frequently took place in the classroom, so that the teacher might draw on incidental happenings meaningful to her own particular children. I saw this happen when a group of seven year olds took cakes they had made to the school kitchen. There the cook welcomed them, allowing them to place their cakes in her oven. Going back to the classroom these children paused to watch the milkman

---

[1] Loukes, Harold, *Friends and Their Children*, Harrap 1958, p. 34.
[2] Robinson, Ruth, 'Prayer in Childhood', *Learning for Living*, SCM Press, Vol. 4, No. 1, September 1964.

unloading the crates of milk bottles, commenting on what they had seen to their teacher. Later in the morning at worship-time the teacher recalled the children's thoughts to these incidents. They, in turn, thought of other people who helped them in school-time: the traffic warden, the bus driver, the caretaker and the dinner helpers. It was suggested that some of the children might care to contribute to a book in which drawings, showing the ways in which these people help, might be placed alongside a prayer of thanksgiving. The teacher followed up the theme by telling a series of stories concerning these and other people who serve the community.

Human relationships

As well as discoveries of relationships between things in the world around them, children have been seen to be discovering themselves and other people. The importance of self-discovery for religious education is obvious, since a child's

> . . . Ultimate religious judgment on the world will depend on his answers to two questions. 'Is this a world that is made for goodness? And does this world want *me* in it?' Both these questions can be discussed in metaphysical terms, and it is the business of theology to deal with the complex issues that can be raised. But religious attitudes do not spring for most men (if, indeed, they do for any) from metaphysical argument; they spring from experience. And if in childhood we discover a world arbitrary and unmanageable, that does not seem to want us very much, then the set of the soul is towards the wrong answers.[1]

Children's conceptions of the deity are in the first place founded on human relations, for only so can they come to know the meaning of such qualities as love and forgiveness, underlying the idea of God as Father. How important human relationships may be is illustrated by a five year old's reaction when told by his teacher that he belonged to God. Returning home he asked his mother to write a letter to God. When his mother asked him why, he said: 'Miss . . . told us we belonged to God. You write him a letter and tell him I don't belong to him, I belong to you and Daddy.' This true story needs no comment.

Though Nathan Isaacs was right when he suggested that 'the child is architect of his own growth',[2] it can also be seen, as Isaacs

---

[1] Loukes, Harold, op. cit., p. 54.   [2] Op. cit., p. 7.

would concur, that the quality of a child's growth will in large measure be dependent upon the quality of the grown-ups who share in his life, for all understanding must grow within the framework of human relationships. In his thesis on the development of religious thinking Ronald Goldman points out that

> . . . Where a teacher shows attitudes of reverence for the wonderful and mysterious world of Nature, shares enjoyment of simple pleasures, appreciates the work of people who help us and naturally shows her dependence upon God, all this must considerably affect the child and begin to create a frame of reference, even if it is primarily emotional.[1]

Many times when visiting infant schools I have witnessed ways in which adult attitudes were unconsciously promoting growth towards a grasp of religious and scientific truth. During one morning it happened thus:

> Five year old Fiona, who had not fully established herself in school, was given a feeling of security as her teacher permitted her to hold her hand as she wandered from group to group.

> Seven year old Jeremy was helped by his teacher to overcome disappointment brought about by failure to make the train he had set his heart on creating. Encouragement and suggestion led to ultimate success.

> Six year old Elspeth's teacher suggested that she and Elspeth together should try to make good the damage caused by Elspeth's carelessness in upsetting water over Sharon's painting.

> Peter, a very intelligent seven year old, was prompted to further enquiry and discovery about birds in which he had become interested by the stimulation of his teacher's queries, which caused him to seek for a more precise interpretation of his personal observations by reference to books.

> Rachel and Jill, both six years, had a disagreement and appealed to their teacher, who listened patiently to both sides of the argument.

> Seven year old Mark was shown by his teacher how to handle tenderly a mother hamster.

> Six year old Mary's wonder over a bunch of brightly coloured dahlias she had brought to school was shared by her teacher.

[1] Goldman, Ronald, *Religious Thinking from Childhood to Adolescence*, p. 232.

Through these teachers the children were coming to know something of the meaning of security, forgiveness, reverence for life, acceptance of difficulties, appreciation of other people's point of view, and the need for penetrating enquiry, bases underlying religious and scientific truth.

If we are to help young children towards a personal discovery of truth we must be content to wait on inner growth, yet at the same time provide opportunities which will foster development, anticipating, but not imposing the formulation of conceptions. We must be sensitive to seize the moment when instruction or suggestion from us will promote further understanding. A. J. Tessimond described the teacher's function when he suggested that

> Man can be taught perhaps only
> That which he almost knows,
> For only in soil that is ready
> Grows the mind's obstinate rose
> > The right word at the wrong time
> > Is wind-caught, blown away;
> > And the most that the ages' sages'
> > Wisdom and wit can say
> Is no more to the quickest pupil
> Than a midwife's delicate steady
> Fingers aiding and easing
> The thought half-born already.[1]

If we accept the need for growth from within, we shall encourage young children to develop their sense perception and shall, at the same time, recognize their emotional needs. Thus, they may not only be helped towards the intellectual and analytical aspects of scientific enquiry, but may sense something of that mystical and unifying vision which is an experience of personal revelation:

Man is born with the religious capacity as with every other. If only his sense for the profoundest depths of his own nature is not crushed out, if only all fellowship between himself and the Primal Source is not quite shut off, religion would, after its own fashion, infallibly be developed.[2]

[1] Tessimond, A. S. J., 'The Deaf Animal', from *Selection*, Putnam 1958.
[2] Schleiermacher, *Discourses on Religion*, trans. by J. Oman, London 1893, Discourse 124.

2 *The Junior School Years*

Personal exploration of the world around

THE DISCUSSIONS and questions of the junior children show a lively curiosity in the world about them which may afford openings for both religious and scientific education, as well as points where integration may take place. Television was a medium whereby children gained much sound knowledge, but it also seemed responsible for a tendency to regard 'science' in some isolation from reality. The science fiction viewed on television and in comics, for instance, fostered a negative attitude on the part of some children, resulting in a type of fantasy thought in which meaningless horror predominated. This was illustrated in the comments made by the two eleven year old boys on their drawings which were entitled 'Invasion from outer space' and 'If war should come' (p. 78). Their attitude seemed to indicate the truth in J. B. Conant's opinion when he asked the question

> . . . Is it not because we have failed to assimilate science into our western culture that so many feel spiritually lost in the modern world? So it seems to me. Once an object has been assimilated, it is no longer alien; once an idea has been absorbed and incorporated into an integrated complex of ideas, the erstwhile, foreign intruder becomes an element of strength. And in this process of assimilation, labels may well disappear. When what we now roughly designate as science has been fully assimilated into our cultural stream, we shall perhaps no longer use the word as we do today.[1]

Older junior children, in particular, seem to need to realize the positive contribution science may make towards an understanding

[1] Conant, J. B., *On Understanding Science*, Mentor Book 1951 edition, p. 18.

of the world in which they live and its relationship with religion. Their own desire to learn of origins and to explore the resources of their immediate surroundings offer channels through which children themselves may enter into the experience of discovery. They have been seen to be as eager as the younger children to enter into personal exploration of things and materials in their environment, becoming intrigued by the problems presented, which prompt further penetration through action or pertinent question. But compared with the younger children their increased experience and developing skill enable them to tackle more complex problems, arriving at more precise solutions. Reference back to the experimental activities with magnets (p. 59) or James Kenward's account of the evolution of the improvised musical instruments (p. 65) gives evidence of this fact.

The same characteristic zest for learning can be seen to enter into their acceptance of the challenge presented by natural forces, which calls for the discipline of developing physical and thinking skills, as in swimming and constructive activities such as building of dams and tree-houses. Their keen interest in plant and animal life opens another avenue for experience, which will arouse both scientific and religious enquiries. Harold Loukes, discussing nature study in education, points out the weaknesses that may occur in both a scientific and religious approach. He suggests how these may be avoided so that further thought and enquiry is fostered:

Nature study is devitalized when it appears as science without religion or religion without science. The offence of science is to fly from wonder and substitute classification. The naming of parts and the collection of species does nothing, by itself, to reveal the miracle of growth. What is needed is a richly varied experience of plant and animal life, by study in a real setting, pond and field rather than diagram and preserving-jar.

The offence of religion is to introduce first causes in the place of immediate causes. The question 'Where did all those bluebells come from?' is not properly answered with 'God put them there'; the wonder of their growth lies in the mechanism of production, and of lying hidden through the year until the spring returns. If an unusually persistent questioner presses us back to 'Who put the first bluebells in the wood?' we may confess that there is still much in nature that we do not understand, saying something of the mystery of creation, and of how we see signs of God at work in this intricacy and order, but are far from knowing just how it has all come about. This kind of answer is better than 'God did', because it is an answer that sets the mind looking forward. It leaves alive the sense of mystery, instead of killing it; and leaves the questioner looking at the point where his knowledge stops, instead of closing his mind by a pronouncement which puts an end to thought.[1]

Experiences such as those envisaged by Harold Loukes permit children to enter into the kind of problems encountered by a scientist in attempting to unveil mysteries. Children may then be better able to comprehend science as a painstaking activity in which men must constantly revaluate their findings in the light of fresh knowledge, and devise more refined tools and techniques to penetrate the mysteries that baffle them. The way may then be opened for children to sense the religious significance of a scientist's work, for as Alan Richardson says:

> . . . the scientist by his patient search for and devotion to truth—whatever he may say with his lips or imagine that he believes with his mind—is really witnessing to the being of God, to the existence of permanent and absolute values, and to the fact that there is purpose and meaning in human existence. The claim which we all recognize that truth has upon us is an intimation of the reality of God and of his presence within our souls; our sense of obligation, which truth imposes upon us, is in fact due to the pressure of God upon our lives, even though we may not have learnt to call him by his proper name. It is the beginning of the knowledge of God within us, our own personal point of contact with him.[2]

A sense of the mysterious

A sense of mystery often accompanies the exercise of curiosity and reasoning in junior children's activities. It was present in the feeling of suspense created by the descent of the paper parachutes at James Kenward's prep school: he recalls that 'the hush that it created was akin to the hush accompanying actual snow'.[3] It was certainly present in many children's questions.

> It puzzles me how God can be in one part of the world, like being here and being in Africa at the same time.
> Why don't the stars fall down?
> How does the light come on when you turn on the switch?

[1] Op. cit., pp. 60-61.
[2] Richardson, Alan, *Science, History and Faith*, OUP 1950, pp. 9-10.
[3] Op. cit., pp. 82-83.

How do cows grow calves?
How do colours of sunrise and sunset get into the sky?
How does a flower grow, when you can't see it happening?
What makes the picture come on the television screen?

Some of these enquiries show how a sense of mystery may be aroused in children through the experience of man-controlled forces, as a memory of a childhood experience related by C. Day Lewis indicates. He recalls how he '. . . first became acquainted with the most mysterious noise of my young life—the sound of telegraph poles humming to themselves, drowsily all through the day'. So deep was the impression that years later it emerged in a sonnet

> It is the humming pole of summer hazes
> Whose sound quivers like heat-haze endlessly
> Over the corn, over the poppied plains
> An emanation from the earth or sky.[1]

From a simple childhood experience he had

> . . . felt what'er there is of power in sound
> To breathe an elevated mood, . . .[2]

But the modern child's environment is far more crammed than C. Day Lewis's childhood world with mysteries concerned with man-controlled forces. This fact is too little recognized in religious education today, for children's interest in such things as television, electricity, aeroplanes, satellites and radar arouses a sense of the mysterious which should surely present opportunities for the integration of religious and scientific attitudes. This need—perceived by M. L. Jacks in 1939—is even more urgent twenty-five years later:

> The scientific 'explanation' of life explains nothing; it is concerned solely with the 'how' and does not attempt to deal with the 'why': it is interested in phenomena, and in cause and effect, but not in meaning: it aims at control, but not at understanding—indeed, it seems that the more it controls, the less it understands, and the dangers of control without understanding are patent to us all today. Science is analytic, religion synthetic—and man needs both, and each needs the other: we must analyse in order that we may control, and we must synthesize in order that we may understand: science needs religion to explain its results, and religion needs science to save it from childishness.[3]

[1] Lewis, C. Day, *The Buried Day*, Chatto and Windus 1960, p. 42.
[2] Wordsworth, William, *The Prelude*, J. M. Dent 1940, Book II, 304-305.
[3] Jacks, M. L., *God in Education*, Rich and Cowan 1939, pp. 73-74.

Previous quotations from autobiography have illustrated how an awareness of reality may come through experiences in the natural world. Sometimes contact with elemental forces may arouse a feeling of deep inexplicable uneasiness like that felt by the boy Wordsworth when

> Scudding away from snare to snare, I plied
> That anxious visitation, hurrying on,
> Still hurrying, hurrying onward; moon and stars
> Were shining o'er my head: I was alone,
> And seemed to be a trouble to the peace
> That dwelt among them.[1]

William Walsh has pointed out that the kind of fear described by Wordsworth was not destructive in its nature but held that element of awe which is the beginning of wisdom, for

> The essential mark of this kind of fear is the liquefaction of set limits or the disturbance of accepted amalgams. Boundaries are upset, eyes blurred, different orders of being flow in upon one another, and the ordinary conceptual pattern of the universe is shattered.[2]

In an age paralysed by a negative dread we must recognize children's need to experience the creative influence which fear may wield. There is, for example, a need to counterbalance the influence underlying the eleven year old boys' conception of the future in the drawings which depicted invasion from outer space and future war (p. 77). That children themselves seek to break through the meaningless dread to more positive conceptions is indicated in some of their spontaneous enquiries, like that of ten year old June who asked: 'Why do we have to blow each other up? Why can't we have peace? There *must* be some way.' Such questions present a challenge, for by helping children to think their way through the problems they raise, fear may become a creative force in the deepening of their thought and enquiry. Wordsworth recognized the contribution made by dread to the growth of the spirit in childhood:

> Fair seed-time had my soul, and I grew up
> Foster'd alike by beauty and by fear.[3]

[1] Wordsworth, William, *The Prelude*, J. M. Dent 1940, Book 1, 313-317.
[2] Walsh, William, *Autobiographical Literature and Educational Thought*, Leeds University Press 1959, p. 10.
[3] Wordsworth, William, *The Prelude*, Book 1, 301-302.

Here may be mentioned Margaret Langdon's account of a children's discussion about fear in which a negative attitude was dominant, similar to that inherent in the eleven year old boys' comments on their pictures, 'If war should come' and 'Invasion from Outer space'. In writing arising from this discussion one girl illustrated how 'With childlike eyes of wisdom they could see the futility but they felt powerless to do anything but accept the situation'.[1]

> The trouble in the world today is caused by fear
> One country fears another
> Because of atom bombs
> Or outer space missiles.
> Its daft I think.
> They spend money on weapons
> And have no money left
> To clothe and feed the people.
>
> Dianne Strutt[2]

One boy, however, showed how he was feeling and thinking his way through to a positive attitude.

> Years before He was born
> People thought He would come to save them.
> When He was born
> Kings came to worship Him.
> He grew up in poverty
> And was betrayed
> For thirty pieces of silver.
> He died.
> And three days later, rose again.
> His life was an example of how love conquers fear.
> But the scientists of today
> Make bombs,
> Lots of bombs
> To blow each other up, and prove themselves
> The better men.
>
> John White[3]

Although concerned with children of secondary school age, Margaret Langdon's description of her work has a message for all teachers concerned with religious and scientific education.

---

[1] Langdon, Margaret, *Let the Children Write*, Longmans, Green 1961, pp. 25-28.
[2] Ibid., p. 26.   [3] Ibid., p. 28.

A sense of the 'numinous'

There seem occasions when the mysterious may cause children to become conscious of eternal realities beyond phenomena. Anne Treneer describes such a moment which occurred when she and her brother were on a blackberry picking expedition. A sudden consciousness of beauty and awe combined to awaken a sense of what Otto called 'the numinous'.[1]

> It must have been September, a hot close day, with a Cornish seamist, and spiders' webs on the furze bushes. We wandered and played, and ate blackberries, and picked others for our basket, going ever farther afield to find 'toppers' . . . We could hear the sea moving quietly below, but we could not see it and the gulls were in the mist. And then we saw a wonderful sight. I suppose the sun was trying to come out and that the rays were in some way refracted by the mist. We saw a golden light, not brilliant, but mellow and suffused, yet with a core of concentrated splendour—a sheaf of gilding. It was the dull yet glowing gold of gilded missals . . . On Dodman Point, on that day of my childhood, I thought the splendour was God. Capnn was not sure that it wasn't. We stole home with no further eyes for 'toppers'.[2]

Anne Treneer and her brother had been brought up in a knowledge of God. Children who have been denied religious instruction may also have a sense of the mysterious from which may spring a sense of 'otherness'. This is evident in an instance quoted by William James in which a spontaneous drive towards the discovery of an originating power is seen in the recollections of a deaf and dumb boy. Though he had had no lessons until eleven years of age, he had, nevertheless, been formulating his own conceptions, of which he later wrote:

> . . . I began to ask myself the question: How came the world into being? When this question occurred to my mind, I set myself thinking it over a long time . . . I believed the sun and moon to be round, flat plates of illuminating matter; and for those luminaries I entertained a sort of reverence on account of their power of lighting and heating the earth. I thought from their coming up and going down, travelling across the sky in so regular a manner that there must be a certain something having power to govern their course.[3]

[1] Otto, Rudolph, *The Idea of the Holy*, Pelican 1959.
[2] Op. cit., pp. 39, 40.
[3] James, William, *Principles of Psychology*, Vol. 1, Longmans, Green 1922, pp. 266-8.

A remarkable account of a boy's spontaneous search for an origin of causes is contained in a record quoted by Pierre Bovet of an experiment in the eighteenth century in which a father brought up his son in isolation from religious ideas. Moreover, all instruction in the boy's first ten years was entirely oral, so that he neither read nor heard of God. The boy later wrote of his reactions to his upbringing, revealing how he searched for a source of causation beyond mankind.

It is interesting to compare this boy's response with that of five year old Alison's story about the little girl who 'wanted to praise the sun because it was shining bright' (p. 36).

My father was anxious to know if there existed in man, over and above the rational disposition, the disposition to a notion of God. Such was the motive underlying the education he gave me . . . I remember very exactly that I used to look upon the sun as the cause of everything that men were unable to perform, but which nevertheless happened. Whenever I could not attribute something to my father, or to other men, I attributed it to no other than the sun . . . Thus in reality, the sun was for me, God, though I did not know the word, 'God' . . .

. . . My father noticed it and was happy . . . He left me to my own devices for a long time. At last he came across me kneeling in the garden with my hand extended towards the rising sun, and thought that the time had come to put an end to my honest errors . . . He took advantage of a clear night at the time of the new moon; making me contemplate the majesty of the starry heavens, he told me only that the innumerable stars I saw were, with but a few exceptions, suns themselves, perhaps even greater than the sun. It was . . . as if someone had dealt me a deadly blow. It was ended now, all my veneration for the sun, and I did not know where to direct the worship I had hitherto devoted to the sun . . .

My father acted as if he had noticed nothing: he went on to give me correct astronomical knowledge, I listened as if I were listening to God Himself. And, in reality, it was to Him I was listening without clearly recognizing it. The startling connection between the infinitude of the universe and a single unit made a deep impression on me. There stirred in me a question which I had not been able to ask when hearing him speak of the innumerable multitudes of suns because I then knew nothing of the relation which bound them into a single unity. What then happened in the end? One clear moonlight night, when my father led me once more into the garden, and made me repeat to him all that I had learned of the heavens and added further information, the question born deep within me presented itself with urgency: 'My father, dear father, you have lowered the sun in my eyes. It was to him that I attached myself. It was he I believed gave us light and happiness and blessed me and all other things. All those millions and myriads of suns up there must stand in some inexpressible relation—there must be *one* . . . Tell me, tell me, who all these suns are . . . who? . . . or why? Then my father intervened, telling me of the Sun of all suns, the original Sun, unique, invisible and eternal cause of the bond between the suns, who did not Himself dwell in any of the suns thus bound together. Hardly had he spoken when I threw myself on his neck, together we fell on our knees. From that moment I became as happy as I had formerly been, even happier. I had the impression, too, that I was wiser than I had ever been, and could not conceive that it was possible to be wiser.[1]

Such a response suggests the truth of Schleiermacher's assertion that

In the relations of man to this world there are certain openings into the Infinite, prospects past which all are led that their sense may find its way into the Whole.[2]

Emotional attitudes

The importance of emotional attitudes cannot be over-emphasized and the junior years are critical in this respect. The children's attitudes to science have already been mentioned, including the tendency to isolate it from religion. As analytical processes are introduced to children we have a responsibility to keep alive the natural awareness of an ultimate mystery:

I see them now across a void
Wider and deeper than time and space.
All that I have come to be
Lies between my heart and the rose,
The flame, the bird, the blade of grass.
The flowers are veiled;
And in a shadow-world, appearances
Pass across a great *toile vide*
Where the image flickers, vanishes,
Where nothing is, but only seems.

[1] Quoted by Bovet, Pierre, in *The Child's Religion*, trans. by G. M. Green, Dent 1928, p. 73.
[2] Op. cit., *Discourses* 130.

But still the mind, curious to pursue,
Long followed them, as they withdrew
Deep within their inner distances,
Pulled the petals from the flowers,
        the wings from flies,
Hunted the heart with a dissecting-knife
And scattered under a lens the dust of life;
But the remoter, stranger
Scales iridescent, cells, spindles, chromosomes
Still merely are;
With hail, snow-crystals, mountains, stars,
For in the dusk, lightning, gnats in the evening air
They share the natural mystery
Proclaim I AM, and remain nameless.[1]

If emotion is tempered with reason, children will be able to enter into that deepest kind of knowing which springs from an exercise of '. . . the whole concourse of mental powers in co-operative action, feeling which energizes reason and reason which enlightens feelings'.[2]

Attitudes towards religious instruction

The general feeling among the junior children—especially the older ones—regarding religious instruction was one of boredom and a sense of unreality, though they felt some guilt when admitting it. The number of junior children interviewed during the period of this study was limited, but memories of more than one hundred students, as well as references in autobiography, confirm the impression. For example, a nineteen year old girl recalling her idea of Jesus wrote:

During the junior school I went through a phase when I regarded him as being far too perfect to be true and rather effeminate and in fact rather a 'cissy'. This was probably due to the way in which he was portrayed in lessons. By this time I realized that he was a man as well as a little boy but not really the sort one could make into a hero.

Such a limited view of the nature of Jesus was frequently expressed in student recollections, for he was invariably pictured as a kind,

[1] Raine, Kathleen, 'Exile', in *The Collected Poems of Kathleen Raine*, Hamish Hamilton 1956.
[2] Walsh, William, *Autobiographical Literature and Educational Thought*, Leeds University Press 1959, p. 12.

gentle healer and a friend, but mention of his courageous qualities was negligible. On the other hand, a few students had vivid memories of how during the junior years Jesus took on a fresh significance. As Richard Church has written: 'The character, the very physical person of Jesus began to loom up as a constant acquaintance.'[1] He goes on to relate how Jesus

> . . . became a companion of my long days at home, and we talked together as freely as though he were a member of the small family; more freely, indeed, for here was somebody who, like Mother, held some mysterious power, some pull of the blood: without, however, letting it slacken through sickness, preoccupation or other mortal deterrent.[2]

The main impression gained from student recollections with regard to biblical material, however, was that it became marred by constant repetition and was not usually seen as being related to life today. The emotional attitude established was, in fact, a rather sentimental one. This was also reflected in the way in which practices concerned with religion were carried out in secret, for example, Bible reading. Such evidence, which is again supported by the findings of Ronald Goldman's research[3] with regard to mental development, indicates that though juniors may be more ready than the younger children to appreciate biblical literature, including references to the life of Jesus, we would be wise to delay the examination of much biblical material if we desire a later mature and positive attitude. The juniors' desire to accumulate factual knowledge and seek for origins, however, may be a means of gaining a background as a setting for future thought and enquiry through an experiential approach.[4]

Children need to be introduced in the junior school years to that 'Vision of Greatness' whereby they can see truth in action in the lives of men. This may include reference to the Bible as a dramatic record of man's search for meaning.

> We ought . . . to help our pupils to enter, through literature and history, into their heritage of the best that has been thought and felt

[1] Church, Richard, *Over the Bridge*, Heinemann 1955, p. 129.
[2] Ibid., p. 129.   [3] Op. cit.
[4] See *Experience and Worship*, Religious Education Press 1963; Goldman, Ronald, *Readiness for Religion*, Routledge and Kegan Paul; Goldman, Ronald (ed.), *Readiness for Religion series*, Rupert Hart-Davis 1965.

and done in the world. The vision alone is not enough. The world needs not only vision but faith. But faith cannot be manufactured. What we can do is to expose ourselves and our pupils to the great sources of inspiration, so that from the vision faith may grow.[1]

Since inspiration and emotional attitudes may also come through music and art, we need to be scrupulous about the quality of that presented to the children. We need also to recognize that, together with drama and movement, music and art may be a means whereby junior children can express their own interpretations often too difficult to communicate in words. By forcing children to express themselves verbally we may easily substitute verbalism for sincerity, thus sacrificing emotional and intellectual integrity. It has been truly stated that 'Language is always tempted to make reality more articulate than it is'.[2]

Human relationships

The development of physical and thinking skills can be seen to bring about in the junior years a growing awareness of self and other people. The significance of this in the growth of a sense of personal responsibility has already been illustrated as, for example, in Frank Kendon's account of the consciousness of his own powers of destruction and sympathetic imagination (p. 85). The importance of a school community in which junior children can think through problems of human relationships has been made clear in the questions and discussions of children. It is fundamental to the growth of both religious and scientific thought.

Worship, as the centre of community living, should be seen by the children as an integral part of their search for meaning in the relationships of things and people. Memories of students frequently mention that junior school worship was more an imposed rather than a living experience and that conceptions of prayer and the Bible were frequently divorced from reality. A consideration of the attitudes expressed suggests that serious thought should be given to this aspect of school-life.

The function of the adult in promoting both religious and scientific thought and enquiry in the junior child seems to be primarily

[1] Jeffreys, M. V. C., *Glaucon*, Pitman 1961 edition, p. 7.
[2] Steere, Douglas, *Where Words Come From*, George Allen and Unwin 1955, p. 48.

. . . to open up for him more and more paths by which his present understanding and his powers of future integration can continue to *grow*.[1]

Observation of children shows how this may come about in the junior years by presenting them with opportunity to make their own discoveries and stresses the fact that misconceptions are inevitable if we are premature in our instruction. It is essential that children experience the ideas on which our conceptions of God are founded before they can come to understanding. At the same time the adult has a responsibility to give instruction which may help children in their interpretation of their experience. Such instruction should be imparted in a way that will enable them to be finally free to make their own judgments.

Ultimately, however, an awareness of reality beyond phenomena to which an understanding of normal experience at fullest depth may lead is something that cannot be taught. Martin Buber has suggested the subtle nature of a child-teacher relationship which may make it possible for children both to grow towards God and to experience how God may reach out to them:

. . . if the educator of our day has to act consciously he must nevertheless do it 'as though he did not'. That raising of the finger, that questioning glance, are his genuine doing. Through him the selection of the effective world reaches the pupil. He fails the recipient when he presents this selection to him with a gesture of interference. It must be concentrated in him; and doing out of concentration has the appearance of rest. Interference divides the soul in his care into an obedient part. But a hidden influence proceeding from his integrity has an integrating force.

The world has its influence as nature and as society on the child. He is educated by the element, by air and light and the life of plants and animals, and he is educated by relationships. The true educator represents both; but he must be to the child as one of the elements.[2]

Thus children through experience of the world about them and through human relationships may come to the discovery that in the search for meaning there is mystery that cannot be solved, yet

[1] Isaacs, Nathan, op. cit., p. 36.
[2] Buber, Martin, *Between Man and Man*, Routledge and Kegan Paul 1947, p. 90.

. . . we may learn to live with it more and more significantly, to
penetrate more and more profoundly its nature, but however deeply
we enter into it and discern its secrets the mystery remains mysterious.[1]

[1] Marcel, Gabriel, *Philosophy of Existence*, Harvill Press 1948.

Appendices

Appendix A

CHILDHOOD REMEMBERED BY STUDENTS AND WRITERS

Childhood remembered by students

The views described here were expressed in optional discussions which were the outcome of students' concern about the religious conceptions of young children. As a recall of childhood memories had been found helpful in previous attempts to understand the view of young children the students thought it might be a useful starting-point on this occasion. A measure of control entered into the pattern of the discussions, since, in answer to a student's spontaneous preliminary enquiry as to what was meant by 'religious conceptions', it was considered that they concerned ideas of God and Jesus, prayer, the Bible and death and heaven. Inevitably, in the course of such a discussion the question of religious education through home, school and church arose, which in turn led to a consideration of the influence of individual people on the formation of attitudes and concepts. The following account represents a summary of the salient features recorded in anonymous notes made after the discussion by about sixty of the one hundred students who participated.

Ideas of God and Jesus were discussed freely, a contribution by one person often quickening the memories of others. To the majority, God had appeared as a kind of superior human being, often possessing supernatural qualities, for he was imagined as all-powerful, all-seeing and omnipresent, which probably accounted for a tendency to regard him in terms of a giant-like physique. On the other hand, there was also evidence that he was sometimes identified with an actual person known to the child, either a near relative (for example, grandfather) or a type of person such as a king. His posture formed a part of many images, for he was frequently pictured as sitting on some kind of throne, or standing with arms outstretched. A few, however, imagined him as being suspended mysteriously by cloud-like forces, and some ascribed to him a dual nature which invested him with a magical power enabling him to remain invisible on earth, whilst visible in heaven. To other minds he had been a partial figure, composed only of head and shoulders, and there were a few memories of a shadowy impression of a 'somebody somewhere called God'. Others could recall no human image but had a vague recollection of a deity associated with light, sun or clouds.

Human moods were attributed to God, the adjectives used being stern, angry and kind, with a prevalence of the former. Though he was considered by some as creator of the universe, his moral nature seemed to be the most prominent characteristic, in that he was often regarded as disliking 'naughty children', sometimes recording misdeeds and demanding to be appeased by means of prayer. There was some evidence that ideas of God changed during the junior years. Alongside the appearance of doubts about the deity there was a growing awareness of 'conscience'. Children with no religious home background found their curiosity in the nature of God quickened towards the end of the junior years. It took considerable courage on the part of a few to 'dare God' by committing some misdemeanour which was believed likely to call forth his anger. Placing something on top of a Bible, or committing idolatry by praying to a chair, were two instances.

The influence of pictures seemed to be reflected in some of the ideas of God, but was most obvious in conceptions of Jesus, who was generally preferred. To most, Jesus had been a shepherd-like figure, described as gentle, kind, loving, and quiet. He was often thought of as being interested in animals, the influence of pictures here being likely. Arising from stories of the miracles, he was thought to possess 'magical' powers and the idea of his divinity caused bewilderment. Whereas some had thought of his as a perfect man, remote because his life was unrelated to human failings, there were others who had regarded him with a degree of sympathy: as a boy as mischievous as themselves who lived in a house in the sky with an exceptionally strict father. Little mention was made of the nativity stories but generally Jesus was thought to be friendly towards children, and a number could remember making him a confidant: one girl recalling how she talked to him as she did to her spaniel. It was again noted that in a few instances where no religious training had been given in the home, the child became interested in the person of Jesus at the end of the primary school years.

God and Jesus were both thought to live in heaven, a place in the sky regions imagined in concrete terms of the human environment, which included the provision of houses and beautiful gardens. The usual picture-type of angel populated this imagined place, and animals were often part of the scene. There were a few exceptions in which vague ghost-like 'souls' took the place of the more concrete angels.

Heaven was also the place to which dead people went and many were the conjectures as to how the transport took place. Many students found it difficult to recollect ideas of death, and where these were most vivid they were concerned with the death of someone beloved. Death was identified with the act of 'going away' or 'going out of sight', some recalling the anguish suffered through an unvoiced fear of losing parents, particularly mother. Where recollections referred to early years they suggested that the child did not associate death with herself, but as the realization that she might die dawned, an anxiety was some-times set up. This fear was dispelled in instances where the child felt able to express her fears to a sympathetic adult. One girl recalled carrying out the cleansing ritual of washing her hands as soon as pos-sible after seeing a funeral, the very word 'death' being regarded in the nature of a taboo.

The first impact with the finality of death came to some through the loss of a pet, which caused speculation about whether the animal would 'go to heaven with God'. The carrying out of solemn burial rites was quite often remembered in connection with the death of animals, and it was through an experiment with caterpillars that one child was convinced about the fact of an after-life. Finding some caterpillars in a curled up state of coma, considered by her to be dead, she and a friend covered them over with leaves and compost in the garden. A few days later the children uncovered the victims to discover a company of wriggling creatures—proof enough to satisfy them of the validity of belief in resurrection.

It was natural that such discussion should incorporate references to ideas of prayer. To many, childhood prayer had been utterly meaning-less, but a few had found it a means of comfort. Though prayers had been addressed to God and Jesus, the latter was generally assumed to be more kindly disposed to the supplicant. 'Gentle Jesus', 'The Lord's Prayer', and 'Jesus, tender Shepherd, hear me', were the three prayers mentioned as having been learned by heart. All to whom the idea of prayer had been introduced at home remembered the list of people whom they asked God to bless. Requests for material things and petitions for fine weather for outings were usually included, mention quite often being made of a bargaining element in the prayer situation. There were instances where 'belief' in adolescence had been founded upon the fact that God had 'completed his side of the bargain'. At the same time, there were indications that some children became puzzled by the nature of the request type of prayer, as they wondered, for example, how God could deal with requests for different kinds of weather at the same time and place.

Although prayers were usually associated with bed-time, school worship, church and Sunday school, there were children who had prayed spontaneously at incidental times, using their own words. In these instances this type of prayer had seemed more real to the child than the formal ritual and was sometimes dissociated from the latter. It was interesting that simple prayer-books incorporating elements of everyday life had given some meaning to prayer where they had been introduced.

Prayer was associated with the common rituals of kneeling and closing of eyes, but as children grew older it became a more secretive affair, and the maintenance of its practice was determined by an element of superstition. Magical beliefs of a compulsive nature were often linked with prayer ritual, such as the effect of length and the need to say them in a certain order.

Similar magical qualities were also attributed to the Bible, which sometimes led to superstitious practices evolved by the child. It was nearly always regarded as having little or no relationship to everyday life, the attitude towards it being tinged with a measure of awe. Though the possession of a Bible was a kind of status symbol, strong feelings of dislike outnumbered the expressions of a positive attitude.

Bibles which were treasured and used by loved adults, such as a mother or grandparent, acquired an aura of significance for a few children. The sensory qualities of the Bible were nearly always mentioned, including the texture and colour of the cover and the pages, the pictures, the gold edges, the zip fastener, together with the importance attached to possessions such as texts and pressed wild flowers kept in the Bible.

A considerable number of students acknowledged that though as children they had a vague notion that the Bible was concerned with God, they really had no idea of its contents and it came as a shock to some when they discovered the Bible was the source of stories they had heard.

Only two remembered appreciating the language of the Bible, the majority recalling anxiety caused by lack of comprehension and subsequent misunderstandings and the negative attitude incurred by being made to learn passages by heart, especially when imposed as a punishment by prefects at secondary school level. A few recorded their great surprise when they eventually discovered that they could understand parts of the Bible. Yet such was the compelling nature of its importance that when a renewed interest was aroused at the beginning of adolescence many were the unsuccessful attempts to read it through.

The ideas mentioned were mainly conveyed through home training, obviously a most powerful influence in establishing attitudes, but school and church also played some part. Many were quite unable to recall religious education in the primary school years, apart from some recollection of stories either enjoyed, or spoiled through constant repetition, and a dislike of learning by heart passages from the Bible which created an attitude of boredom. The Scripture examinations undertaken in Church of England schools were chiefly recalled by the feeling of relief and joy associated with the half-day holiday which followed the event!

Worship was the most commonly remembered experience in the primary school years, but apart from the Festivals, such as Harvest and Christmas, there was little evidence of the establishment of a positive attitude.

Many complained that at the Grammar School level GCE preparation destroyed their interest, though a few had found that a historical approach had quickened their understanding. Where discussion methods had been introduced they were much appreciated, especially when led by a teacher who showed respect for the children's point of view. The people associated with the teaching were of paramount importance at all stages.

Although there were a few exceptions, generally speaking church attendance was recollected as a practice to be endured rather than enjoyed. In early years it was thought of as a place where God and the minister lived, but was chiefly remembered in reference to inhibitions caused by 'best clothes' and the frustrations of sitting still, together with activities invented to relieve the boredom and subsequent reprimands. As with the Bible, deep sensory impressions were responsible for vivid recollections of windows, brass candlesticks, peculiar smells and a special 'ethereal' atmosphere. In a few cases a girl expressed deep appreciation for the work of a Sunday school or church, and this was due to the apparent seriousness with which children's and youth work was regarded. Such seriousness had been fostered where the staff of a Sunday school and youth club had undergone some form of training.

In the church and Sunday school, as in all spheres, positive attitudes were fostered by relationships with adults who were not only concerned about religious instruction but sensitive to the needs of the young.

In the early years the idea of adult infallibility was universal, only gradually did an awareness of imperfections dawn. As the influence of their peers became increasingly important, and the general social climate of the times made its impression, children tended to regard religion as 'cissy'. In the early 'teens, the attitude of teenage idols towards religion was also a powerful influence.

Several interesting points arise from these recollections. On the one hand, there is the quite frequent mention of a change of conception in the junior years. This might involve doubts about God and an awareness of what one student termed the 'greedy nature of prayer', together with a growing feeling that religion and 'gentle Jesus' were for the young. On the other hand, the junior years were also represented as a period when there was a keen curiosity about religious matters. Particularly interesting is the fact that this seemed to occur most forcibly in the lives of children where there was no religious home background.

Childhood remembered by writers[1]

Against the background of the student discussions, reference was made to some twenty autobiographies and extracts relating to the religious conceptions suggested by the students were noted. This treatment of autobiography meant that there was a certain bias in the selection of material. Although it is realized that such a bias prevented an appreciation of other significant material, this limited approach did yield an interesting variety of comparative illustrations. The influence of a later mode of selection will be apparent in the inclusion of a few experiences which exceed the narrower conceptions of the student discussions.

Though references to Jesus were few, ideas of God were frequently mentioned. These included examples of close identification of the deity with a human being, such as father, and the doubt, or relief, which ensued when such idols were found to be fallible. Ideas ranged from images couched in terms of a human being, though sometimes of a semi-fantasy type, to a variety of symbolic ideas represented by light,

[1] Autobiographies referred to are listed on p. 125.

the intangible yet powerful nature of wind, or a vague frightening sense of infinity experienced by one child in a dream.

Opposing opinions concerning God's nature included one which referred to him as indifferent and pitiless, and another which acknowledged a consciousness of his companionship. Generally he was considered as an authority, inclined to be 'magnificently frightening' and capable of anger. One child, who regarded him as the dispenser of both evil and good, thought impartiality to be his chief virtue. The awareness of the moral character of God was sometimes indicated in a child's fear of God's retaliation after a misdeed, such as telling an undetected lie —a fear which might be so intense as to take the form of an overwhelming physical sensation of an avenging presence. The same element of fearsome-awe, which created an awareness of 'otherness', seemed to be inherent in the response of some children in the presence of overpowering or majestic natural phenomena, like a thunderstorm or the eeriness of night-time. This awe, aroused at times by a more common experience like a cuckoo-call, might be strangely mingled with an uncanny pleasure. There were occasions when the beauty of some natural thing caught a child by surprise or the excitement of some discovery about the world, either initiated by self-activity or through an adult, created a kind of affinity with the natural world. Such sensitivity might include, yet outstrip, the bounds of normal sensibility.

In contrast to such sensitivity may be set the fact that there was evidence that a child might exercise reason in, for example, puzzling out God's predicament when faced with conflicting prayer requests, yet at the same time experience relief in a certainty of his dependable nature. Even so, these children resorted to secret magical practices in their private prayer life, which was frequently quoted as being connected with desires for material things. Prayer was also remembered with regard to moral situations, where God's forgiveness was asked. One writer told of the ease with which she confessed an undetected misdeed to God, in comparison with the intense guilt felt towards the adult who had been deceived.

As belief in the infallibility of adults lessened, alongside a greater realization of self, there was a tendency to put God's omnipotence to the test, a feat usually requiring courage. One writer, however, with no religious home background, recalled how with no qualms she firmly renounced the Christian faith at about the age of ten, though she also related how interest in religion was later renewed. Changes in religious conceptions were recorded, these seeming to coincide with the development of a child's self-awareness which included a growth of imaginative sympathy.

Most interesting was the description of a child's anxiety caused by a father's disbelief which led his son to create imaginary evidence of God's existence. The misery caused when confronted with the true facts, which conflicted with his earlier misconception, was a vivid example of the reality of such fantasy interpretation to a child. Curiosity about origins was often mentioned and one queried whether her actions were pre-ordained.

The manner in which religious conceptions of children who had experienced the usual exposure to religious teaching were interpreted in solitary thought and play with others was described by some authors. Numerous misunderstandings were quoted, which arose from a lack of comprehension of biblical language. Feelings of dislike and boredom were often associated with the Bible, though mention was made of the way in which in later childhood a renewed but secretive interest took place, including attempts to read it through. To a few, even in the early days, its language had a compelling magnetic attraction and such children enjoyed memorizing the passages.

Some of the ideas about angels and heaven, though they bore a resemblance to those about 'fairyland', arose also from biblical sources and there was some speculation about the nature of eternity. The impact caused by the death of a loved person was mentioned by a few, but most references to death involved animals. The acceptance of the finality of death seemed to have some affinity with the gradual development of a sense of personal moral responsibility arising from a child's own experience of his own powers of destruction. The transition from an early belief in the permanency of all things to a realization and gradual acceptance of the temporal nature of much in the environment, including self, was also illustrated by experience of the natural world.

The influence of the attitudes of people in the home situation in the forming of conceptions was evident. Very little direct reference was made to religious education in school, church attendance and worship being occasionally mentioned, but the influence of adults was implied. Although Bible readings and hymns and church festivals were sometimes mentioned with appreciation, most references recalled church attendance as an activity to be endured, the outstanding impressions describing people, sensory impressions, games invented to while away the time or the compensating anticipation of a Sunday dinner.

Autobiographical references

Carr, Emily, *The Book of Small*, OUP 1944.
Church, Richard, *Over the Bridge*, Heinemann 1955.
Common, Jack, *Kiddar's Luck*, Turnstile Press 1951.
de la Mare, Walter, *Early One Morning*, Faber and Faber 1935.
Dennis, Geoffrey, *Till Seven*, Eyre and Spottiswoode 1957.
Freeman, Gwendolen, *Children Never Tell*, George Allen and Unwin 1949.
Gosse, Edmund, *Father and Son*, Penguin Books 1949.
Keller, Helen, *The Story of My Life*, Hodder and Stoughton 1947.
Kendon, Frank, *The Small Years*, OUP 1950.
Kenward, James, *Prep School*, Penguin 1961.
Lee, Laurie, *Cider with Rosie*, Penguin 1962.
Lewis, C. Day, *The Buried Day*, Chatto and Windus 1960.
Lewis, Eiluned, *Dew on the Grass*, Peter Davies 1951.
Masefield, John, *So Long to Learn*, Heinemann 1952.

Palmer, Herbert E., *The Mistletoe Child*, J. M. Dent 1953.
Paul, Leslie, *The Living Hedge*, Faber and Faber 1946.
Raverat, Gwen, *Period Piece*, Faber and Faber 1952.
Treneer, Anne, *School House in the Wind*, Jonathan Cape 1950.
Uttley, Alison, *Ambush of Young Days*, Faber and Faber 1937.
Wordsworth, William, *Prelude*, J. M. Dent 1940.
Yeats, W. B., *Autobiographies*, Macmillan 1956.

Appendix B

SIX TO EIGHT YEAR OLDS WRITE
ABOUT GOD

1. Young children's preoccupation with immediate and personal interests was reflected in their choice of topic, when a group of thirty six and seven year olds, who lived in a seaside town, were asked, as an experiment by a student, to write about one of the following three topics:

the sea	(21 children)
the wind	(6 children)
God	(3 children)

The three children who chose to write about God did so as follows:

    (*a*) the wind is God.
    (*b*) God is a man he made the world.
        (Child drew picture of globe-like world with figure of God standing in the sky above.)
    (*c*) God is an invisible person God can see us but we cant see him Gods evrywhere were we are he walks with us evrywhere We go he gos to the bech (beach).
        (This description was accompanied by a drawing of God in the form of a human figure standing in the sky by the sun.)

2. The following is a selection from several sources of children's responses to teachers' suggestion that they might write something which would tell people about God. The children were aged six to eight years of age.

  1. God is a good man he made the erth and the flowers, he made things.
  2. God lives under gound and in the sky when old polpe die they go to Heaven   God makes them better they cannot come back down from the sky and they cannot ris up from the gound.

3. God is Jesus father and when any body dusnt fell very well he helps them to get better
God lives up in the sky and when somebody died they went up in the sky as well

4. God is verey nice man to use he gives us wot we want I like him he is nice because he makes the flowers and the sky and trees the toys and he makes the lovely things we want he made the earth that the flowers grow on he makes the mud that we can plat the seeds in so we love him he sands the good childdren up to heaven and he sands the bad childen down to heven so that we will be good down there and then we will be sant up to heven and the peoppl that are bad down there will stay down there so we love him. he will love us I love him too He must love every one in the whole world so we must as well I love Him he is verey nice and now I must say good bye.

5. God is a brave man. God can make people better who are sick We are Gods children God likes us if we are good

6. Jesus was Gods son God made evrything in the world. He made creachs (creatures) flowers and people God is good so is Jesus. First there was nuthing in the world When God was born it was different.

7. God is a very good man. We are his children. In the bible it tells us about God. God is a brave man. God is in heaven. We sings songs about God, God is very kind to us. Jesus is God's son and he let him do some work.

8. God is a very nice man he had a very Good mind to he maid the flowers and the sky and us to he was nice when he was little to and he was nice to little children becuse he read them lots of storys all out of his own miand and he is very chental (gentle) to over peapol and maid the sun to   he is a very Good man   People love him very much   his mother was called Mary they hadent any sear name when God was a baby Mary loved him very much the cot was very wam to   I think God is very lucky to he helped Mary very much when he was little he helped a bliand man   God was once crosified on a cross and beriad in a cave with very big stones   It is very dark in caves I am skierd of caves my sister is to God is a nice man he is very Good to Mary to   When God was a boy he always is nic.

9. God is King and good   God is very helthy   God is in heven   God was the fist man on erth   God livs in heven

10. The man lives in the sky up in the clouds ever so big his name his God he look after the children

11. The man lives in the sky up in the clouds ever so big his name is God he loves birds and loves children very much.

12. God Lives up in the sky   God make snow.

13. The man Lives in the sky up ever so hiy in the sky and he is big and he can see us down to see wot we arn doing and his name is God.

14. I expect you know God made the would? But you dont know what it was like before God made the world. It was dark, and there was

no land, or people. God said let there be light and there was light,
And God make everything.

15. God Gives us water, food and clothes. He brings the doctor when
we are ill. He makes us love.

16. God I dont want to die Lord keep us till moning. Lord I want to
get married   God lives in heaven every Where   We pray to God

17. God is kind and good to us and he love us and other people as
well and old people as well and if they die God make them well and
good again and if children are ill he makes them better again and
they can walk again and run about again and play gams again.

18. God is Jesus's father   God has a beard and his son is a very good
Healer and God is breaver as a lion and someone is gods mother

19. God looks like a plain man and he has a lot of clothes, And God is
Jesuse's Father. God and Jesus live up in Heaven   And God is
wise and God got marred (married) to Mary   And Then she died
And God does miracles   And God makes peple well again.

20. God is nice and he likes children and he lives in the sky and God is
thirteen and he has a son.

21. God is nice   God wears white   God is very good and is invisible
man and God livs high above the sky   God lics children   God
wears to shoes and God has a sun Jesus . . .

22. God wears a white cloak and He wears a white beard. God is
nice   He wears two shoes   God lives in heven   he loves as (us)
and he made the creatures fat

23. God makes the grass grow and he sends the rain to make evrything
grow and he wears a beard on his chin and he wears a cloak and
God is Fat God is tall and he a son called Jesus and he sends the
sun and he makes the food and he is in heaven and he makes
children and Mothers and Fathers.

24. God wears white clothes   God is the holy Ghost   God is Love
God Likes me   GodS star is the biggest star every Christmas is
GodS Birthday   he is more than 1000 years old.

25. God has a beard and He has a white Hood and a cloak on   God
like us and He love are mummys and daddys and He is kind and
He has a friendly head and He is tall and God makes children.

26. God is wonderful and God Has a halo and God Is kind and God
makes The animals and God is the father of Jesus and God makes
the babies And God lives in heaven And has a wife and Her name
is Mary And God makes the grass grow.

27. God is a very important man and God helps us to work hard. And
God helps all the sik people to get better. And he is kind and God
helps us to be kind to each outher and he helps us to be brave And
he helps the birds to sing.

28. God is vary good and he is kind and he givs us Food and he helps
us to be good and he taks all of are lise (our lies) out of are heads
so we do not tele a big laie (lie) and God makes the flowers growe
in the garden and he makes us kind and he make us play fare.

E

29. God send the rain and sun   god helps us to play gentle and sends
    Our food that we eat   god is gentle to us and give us what we want
    and he helps us to work hard at our sums and he helps the children
    in hospital to get better.
30. God is kind and gentle and God gives us food to eat and God is
    round us. And he gave us houses to live in   God helps us to work
    and do what our teachers tell us and God helps us to be good   God
    gives us trees.
31. He send the rain and He is kind to us   He helps us to be good girls
    and boys   He Gives us flowers and birds   He helps us to learn
32. God is nice and he Has a wife called Mary and he was born on
    Christmas morning and he sends the sun and The pets and helps
    us to grow.
33. God helps us make things and he can see us but we cannot see him
    and God made everything and helps us to grow. and he helps the
    flowers to grow. by sending the rain and the sun. and God is a very
    important man and why we can't see him is because he is invisible.
34. He is helpfull   He made all human beings   He was borne in a
    stable   He was Borne on Christmas day that is 25th of December
    He gives us a happy Life   Some times he can make Bad men good
    He gives us water and food.   He makes us stong and He gives us
    wild Life.
35. He send the rain and Sun and He sends evry liveing thing   He send
    the beautiful autum leavs   He is with us all the time but we can not
    see him.
36. God is a spirit and he is kind God made this land and he made
    the autumn and the winter and the summer and the spring for us and
    the leafs and he like us and he makes the homes for us and he make
    the flowers grow and he make us grow up and he makes the apples
    grow and he makes the birds fly.
37. God is good   God helps us   God is kind   He helps us to do our
    work and he is our father he sends the sun and the rain and he
    sends the snow in the winter he sends the flowers in the summer
    God is a gentle man
38. God is kind and he gives us Food and he Makes us grow and he
    likes boys and girls and he gives us chocolat and he gives us bed to.

Appendix C

SOME CHILDREN'S COMMENTS ARISING
FROM BIBLE STORIES

1. Six year olds after being told the Easter story enquired:

How did he die?
We won't rise like that, will we?
How did he rise?
(Another child suggested: a miracle of God)
Is there such a thing as angels? I've never seen them.
When he died his blood washed away the sins of the whole world.
Why aren't angels alive? How did they come?
Could Jesus breathe in the cave?
How could Jesus get through the stone?
How did he get from the cross to the tomb?
What are the marks in his hands? (reference to picture)
Why are the angels in the tomb? (reference to picture)

2. A group of six year olds had been told the Easter stories and their teacher reports

The Easter story aroused keen interest and it appeared that few of the children had any idea of it before, even those who attend Sunday school regularly, which is over half the class. The children had no idea that Jesus was ever in prison or died, and one child said: 'Jesus couldn't be put in prison because he never let anything nasty happen and he always put things right in stories.'

To several of the children Jesus seemed to be merely a means to bring about a 'happy ending'. They often asked for the Easter stories to be repeated, even in the following term. Each time a number of questions were asked and I noticed that there was little informal discussion among the children, the questions being directed to me. The questions were of the following type:

Why did Jesus die?
How could he help anyone by dying?
What happened to Jesus when he died?
What happens to us when we die?
How do we go up to heaven?

One or two children made speculative comments about how people got to heaven. James said: 'I think God will fetch us himself so we won't be frightened,' and Stuart suggested: 'I think we shall float up on a cloud.' At this point, Rosemary, a rather difficult child with a poor home background, commented: 'My mummy says when you are dead they bury you and you turn to dust, so I don't really think you go to heaven at all.' The other children rejected this idea and one child said: 'Don't be silly, if they did that there wouldn't be any of you left to go to heaven at all.'

I cannot recall the exact words of the conversation which followed but it was to the effect that we would not be able to recognize each other without our bodies and there was no conception of a 'soul' apart from the body. They seemed quite satisfied with the idea that we were lifted up bodily and carried to heaven.

Some of the children found it hard to understand why Jesus had to go back to heaven after he had risen from the dead. Andrew said: 'But Jesus is here in this room. Is he in heaven, too? Why can't we see him like his friends did? Surely he could help everyone better if he had stayed here.'

3. The following conversation took place after a class of six year old children had heard the story of Jesus stilling the storm.

Julia	I wonder why they were frightened? I wouldn't have been because Jesus was there.
Stuart	Jesus is here, too, isn't he? I can't see him, though. How do we know he is here?
William	Because he's everywhere. I wonder if somebody is stepping on him?
Julia	How does he go home with all of us? I run, does he keep up with me?
William	He sees where we go. I always run when it's dark because he can't see me. I don't like the dark. If I have a bad dream in the night I get frightened. Can Jesus see me then? I don't think he can. I put the clothes over my head and sometimes I think about Jesus but it doesn't help.
Stuart	Oh yes, he can see you. He must have funny eyes. I wonder what they look like.

4. The following comments were made after six year old Christopher had heard the story of the healing of the ten lepers.

Christopher   Is heaven up in the sky somewhere? Jesus is up
              there, isn't he? What's the matter, why doesn't he
              make anyone better now? I asked him to make me
              better when I was ill but he didn't and I had to wait
              ages for the doctor to do it. Doesn't he know how
              to make people better any more?

5. A group of six- and seven-year-olds, who had been asked to tell
their teacher what they knew about Jesus, made the following comments:

He was born in a stable.
He used to help Joseph in the carpenter's shop.
Herod wanted to kill him. They said he was doing wrong when he
was doing right.
He had a beard and a long robe. It is black, his beard.
He wore a long cloak and sandals or sometimes had bare feet.
He is a good man who made the whole world.
He made people and animals.
He gave us brains.
He gave ideas of building schools and aircraft.
He copied his father.
He's not scared of anything, not even of walking on water.
He was very brave.
When Jesus was walking on the sea it must have been his spirit that
carried him across.
Jesus made people live again. He will make us alive again.
How can you come alive again?
Jesus has got a sort of note book and he writes about you when you
swear.
When you are naughty Jesus puts your name down in a black book.
If you are christened you will go to heaven, if you are buried. If you
are not christened, you won't.

The same teacher asked the children to tell her what they knew about
God, and the following comments were made:

God dresses up as a bogey man so I hide under the sheets in bed.
God is a bogey man dressed up with a stick: he will get you.
He is under the bed dressed in red.
God's magic.
God can see through the sky.
God can see us all the time.
If God came as a spirit, how was he born?
If you opened a door and God were there, you wouldn't be able to
see him if he were white.
He is an invisible thing that makes you work.
When you are buried the devil will be beside you.

Bibliography

Bibliography

Acland, Richard, *We Teach Them Wrong: Religion and the Young*, Gollancz 1963

Adler, Alfred, *What Life Should Mean to You*, Allen and Unwin 1938 edition

Allen, Brown, Southam and Tuke, *Scientific Interests in Children Under Eight*, National Froebel Foundation pamphlet 1960

Anthony, Sylvia, *The Child's Discovery of Death*, Kegan Paul 1940

Barnes, Kenneth, *The Creative Imagination*, Allen and Unwin 1960

Boeke, Kees, *The Children's Workshop Community*, Bilthoven, Holland 1935

Boeke, Kees, *The Cosmic View: The Universe in 40 Jumps*, John Day, N.Y. 1957

Bovet, Pierre, *The Child's Religion*, trans. G. M. Green, Dent 1928

Brown, Lawrence E., *Where Science and Religion Meet*, REP 1950

Buber, Martin, *Between Man and Man*, trans. Ronald Gregor Smith, Kegan Paul 1947

Chaloner, Len, *Feeling and Perception in Young Children*, Tavistock Publications 1963

Chaloner, Len, *Questions Children Ask*, Faber and Faber 1952

Churchill, Eileen, *Counting and Measuring*, Routledge and Kegan Paul 1961

Conant, James B., *On Understanding Science*, Mentor Book 1961 edition

Dewey, John, *Experience and Education*, Macmillan N.Y. 1954 edition

Deutsche, Jean M., *The Development of Children's Causal Relations*, University of Minnesota Press 1937

Elmhirst, L. K., *Rabindranath Tagore*, John Murray 1961

Fletcher, Basil, *A Philosophy for the Teacher*, OUP 1961

Fox, H. W., *The Child's Approach to Religion*, Harper and Row N.Y. 1945 edition

Frankfort, Henri (and others), *Before Philosophy*, Pelican Book 1946

Froebel, Friedrich, *The Education of Man*, Appleton 1887

Furlong, Monica, *With Love to the Church*, Hodder and Stoughton 1965

Gesell, Arnold, and Ilg, Frances L., *The Child from Five to Ten*, Hamish Hamilton 1946

Goldman, Ronald, *Religious Thinking from Childhood to Adolescence*, Routledge and Kegan Paul 1964

Goldman, Ronald, *Readiness for Religion*, Routledge and Kegan Paul 1965

Goldman, Ronald (Ed.), *Readiness for Religion Series*, Rupert Hart-Davis 1965

Griffiths, Ruth, *A Study of Imagination in Early Childhood*, Routledge and Kegan Paul 1935

Hartley, Ruth, Lawrence, K., Goldenson, Robert M., *Understanding Children's Play*, Routledge and Kegan Paul 1952

Haupt, Dorothy, *Science Experiences for Nursery School Children*, National Association for Nursery Education, Chicago 1955

Heckenstall-Smith, Hugh, *Doubtful Schoolmaster*, Peter Davies 1962

H.M.S.O., *Primary Education*, 1959

Hourd, Marjorie, *Some Emotional Aspects of Learning*, Heinemann 1951

Hourd, Marjorie, *The Education of the Poetic Spirit*, Heinemann 1949

Hourd, Marjorie, and Cooper, Gertrude, *Coming into their Own*, Heinemann 1959

Isaacs, Nathan, *Early Scientific Trends in Children*, National Froebel Foundation pamphlet 1960 edition

Isaacs, Nathan, *The Growth of Understanding in the Young Child*, ESA 1961

Isaacs, Susan, *Intellectual Growth of Young Children*, Routledge and Kegan Paul 1948 edition

Isaacs, Susan, *Social Development in Young Children*, Routledge and Kegan Paul 1937

Jacks, M. L., *God in Education*, Rich and Cowan 1939

James, William, *The Varieties of Religious Experience*, Longmans, Green 1922 edition

Jeffares, A. Norman, *Language, Literature and Science*, Leeds University Press 1959

Jeffreys, M. V. C., *Beyond Neutrality*, Pitman 1950

Jeffreys, M. V. C., *Glaucon*, Pitman 1961 edition

Jeffreys, M. V. C., *The Mystery of Man*, Pitman 1957

Jeffreys, M. V. C., *Personal Values in the Modern World*, Pelican 1962

Jersild, Arthur, *Child Psychology*, Staples Press 1960

Jersild, Arthur, *When Teachers Face Themselves*, N.Y. Teachers College, Columbia University 1955

Jersild, A. T., and Tasch, R. J., *Children's Interests*, Bureau of Publications, Columbia University, N.Y. 1949

Jones, Mary Alice, *The Faith of our Children*, Abingdon Press 1943

Jung, C. G., *Modern Man in Search of a Soul*, Kegan Paul, Trench, Trubner 1933

Kitto, H. D. F., *The Greeks*, Pelican Books 1951

Klein, Melanie, *Our Adult World and Its Roots in Infancy*, Tavistock Publications Pamphlet No. 2 1960

Krishnamurti, J., *Education and the Significance of Life*, Gollancz 1955

Langdon, Margaret, *Let the Children Write*, Longmans 1961

Lawrence, Evelyn (edited by), *Friedrich Froebel and English Education*, ULP 1952

Loukes, Harold, *Friends and Their Children*, Harrap 1958

Loukes, Harold, *Teenage Religion*, SCM Press 1961

Lovell, Kenneth, *Educational Psychology and Children*, ULP 1960

Lovell, Kenneth, *The Growth of Basic Mathematical and Scientific Concepts in Children*, ULP 1961

Marcel, Gabriel, *The Philosophy of Existence*, Harvill Press 1948

Mellor, Edna, *Education through Experience in the Infant School Years*, Blackwell 1950

Navarra, John Gabriel, *The Development of Scientific Concepts in a Young Child*, Bureau of Publications, Columbia University, New York 1955

Niblett, W. R., *Christian Education in a Secular Society*, OUP 1960

Niblett, W. R., *Essential Education*, 1947

Niblett, W. R., *Education and the Modern Mind*, Faber and Faber 1954

Opie, Peter and Iona, *The Language and Lore of Schoolchildren*, Clarendon Press 1959

Oraison, Marc, *Love or Constraint* (trans. Una Morrissy), Burns and Oates 1959

Osborn, Andrew R., *Schleiermacher and Religious Education*, OUP 1934

Otto, Rudolf, *The Idea of the Holy*, Pelican Books 1959 edition

Parkhurst, Helen, *Exploring the Child's World*, Appleton-Century Crofts Inc. N.Y. 1951

Peel, E. A., *The Pupil's Thinking*, Oldbourne 1960

Pelz, Werner and Lotte, *God is No More*, Gollancz 1964

Phillips, J. B., *Your God is too Small*, Wyvern Books 1952

Piaget, Jean, *The Child's Conception of the World*, Routledge and Kegan Paul 1960 edition

Piaget, Jean, *The Child's Construction of Reality*, Routledge and Kegan Paul 1955

Piaget, Jean, *The Growth of Logical Thinking from Childhood to Adolescence*, Routledge and Kegan Paul 1958

Piaget, Jean, *The Child's Conception of Geometry*, Routledge and Kegan Paul 1960

Piaget, Jean, *The Child's Conception of Physical Causality*, Routledge and Kegan Paul 1930

Piaget, Jean, *Play, Dreams and Imitation*, Heinemann 1951

Piaget, Jean, *The Moral Judgment of the Child*, Routledge and Kegan Paul 1932

Piaget, Jean, *The Psychology of Intelligence*, Routledge and Kegan Paul 1950

Pilkington, Roger, *World Without End*, Fontana Books 1961

Polanyi, Michael, *The Study of Man*, Routledge and Kegan Paul 1959

Polanyi, Michael, *Science, Faith and Society*, University of Durham: Riddell Memorial Lecture, OUP 1946

Raine, Kathleen, *The Collected Poems of Kathleen Raine*, Hamish Hamilton 1956

Richards, I. A., *Science and Poetry*, Kegan Paul, Trench, Trubner and Co. 1926

Richardson, Alan, *Science, History and Faith*, OUP 1950

Robinson, John A. T., *Honest to God*, SCM Press 1963

Robinson, John A. T., *The New Reformation?*, SCM Press 1965

Rousseau, *Emile*, Extracts trans. Eleanor Worthington, D. C. Heath, Boston 1899

Russell, David H., *Children's Thinking*, Ginn and Co. N.Y. 1956

Smith, J. W. D., *Psychology and Religion in Early Childhood*, SCM Press 1953 edition

Stone, L. Joseph, and Church, Joseph, *Childhood and Adolescence*, Random House N.Y. 1956

Steere, Douglas, *Where Words come From*, George Allen and Unwin 1955

Suttie, Ian D., *The Origins of Love and Hate*, Kegan Paul, Trench, Trubner 1935

Tanner, J. M., and Inhelder, Barbel (Ed.), *Discussions on Child Development*, Volumes I and II, Tavistock Publications 1953 and 1954

Tessimond, A. S. J., *Selection*, Putnam 1958

Thomson, Robert, *The Psychology of Thinking*, Pelican Book 1959

Thorburn, Marjorie, *The Spirit of the Child*, Allen and Unwin 1946

Toulmin, Stephen, *The Philosophy of Science*, Hutchinson 1955

Tournier, Paul, *The Strong and the Weak*, SCM Press 1963

Wall, W. D., *Education and Mental Health*, UNESCO 1955

Walsh, William, *Autobiographical Literature and Educational Thought*, Leeds U.P. 1959

Walsh, William, *The Use of Imagination*, Chatto and Windus 1959

Weaver, Anthony, *They Steal for Love*, Max Parrish 1959

Whitman, Walt, *Complete Verse and Selected Poems*, Nonesuch Press 1938

Yeaxlee, Basil, *Religion and the Growing Mind*, Nisbet 1959